Real Estate Wholesaling

How to Start with Real Estate Wholesaling, from 0 to $100k per Month

TABLE OF CONTENTS

INTRODUCTION 5

CHAPTER 1: WHAT IS REAL ESTATE WHOLESALING? .. 7

    HOW IT WORKS 9
    DIFFERENCE BETWEEN REAL ESTATE WHOLESALING AND
    RETAIL 11
    BENEFITS/ADVANTAGES OF REAL ESTATE WHOLESALING 15
    DISADVANTAGES OF WHOLESALING 18
    IS REAL ESTATE WHOLESALING FOR YOU? 20

CHAPTER 2: REAL ESTATE WHOLESALING STEPS AND WHERE IT WORKS 22

    SIMPLE STEP BY STEP GUIDE ON HOW TO WHOLESALE A REAL
    ESTATE PROPERTY 23
    MISTAKES PEOPLE MAKE WHEN WHOLESALING 31

CHAPTER 3: REQUIREMENTS FOR REAL ESTATE WHOLESALING 37

    FINANCIAL REQUIREMENTS FOR WHOLESALING 40
    THE DO'S AND DON'TS OF REAL ESTATE WHOLESALING 42
    REAL ESTATE WHOLESALING GOALS 51
    WHAT YOU ARE NOT TOLD IN REAL ESTATE WHOLESALING 56

CHAPTER 4: WHOLESALING STRATEGIES AND PROFITS 59

    STRATEGIES 60
    HOW TO MAKE A PROFIT FROM WHOLESALING 70
    HOW TO WHOLESALE WITH $1000 78

CHAPTER 5: GETTING THE RIGHT PROPERTY TO SELL 79

- SINGLE FAMILY HOMES 80
- CONDOS AND TOWNHOMES 83
- MOBILE HOMES 85
- APARTMENT BUILDINGS 86
- COMMERCIAL REAL ESTATE 88
- VACANT LOTS AND LAND..............................89
- HOW TO FIND PROPERTIES FOR WHOLESALE REAL ESTATE INVESTMENT 91

CHAPTER 6: HOW TO GET THE BEST OFFER 101

- TALKING TO SELLERS THE RIGHT WAY 102
- HOW TO IDENTIFY MOTIVATED SELLERS 109
- NEGOTIATING TIPS FOR WHOLESALE REAL ESTATE 113

CHAPTER 7: WORKING WITH THIRD-PARTIES 121

- THE ROLE OF A TITLE COMPANY 121
- HOW MUCH DO YOU PAY? 130
- PRE-PURCHASE INSPECTION 130

CHAPTER 8: RENOVATING THE PROPERTY.............148

- SIGNS THE PROPERTY NEEDS RENOVATING 149
- BENEFITS OF RENOVATING THE PROPERTY 155
- FINANCING PROPERTY RENOVATIONS: WHAT YOU NEED TO KNOW 159
- COST OF HOME RENOVATION 161
- PROPERTY RENOVATION MISTAKES TO AVOID................164
- CHOOSING A CONTRACTOR 167

CHAPTER 9: FINDING THE RIGHT BUYER 170

THE TYPES OF PROPERTY BUYERS YOU WILL ENCOUNTER .. 170
HOW TO CHOOSE THE BEST BUYER FOR YOUR PROPERTY . 177
HOW TO NEGOTIATE FOR A BETTER PRICE FOR YOUR
PROPERTY 183

CHAPTER 10: CLOSING ON THE PROPERTY 191

POOR QUALITY IMAGES 191
LACK OF ENOUGH PROMOTION 192
INCORRECT VALUATION 193
POOR IMPRESSION 194
YOU AREN'T DECIDED 194
POOR COMMUNICATION 195
POOR SERVICE 196
INCREASING RATES AND PRICES 197
THE DECLINE IN MOTIVATED BUYERS 198
CROWDED MARKET 198
HIGH COST OF REPAIRS 199
FINDING THE RIGHT AGENT 200
LOCAL MARKET CONDITIONS 206
UNREALISTIC BUYERS 208
INSPECTIONS 208
CLOSING THE DEAL 209
FINAL THOUGHTS 210

Introduction

Wholesaling is one of the easiest ways of making money from the real estate industry. It allows you to engage in buying and selling properties without necessarily owning them.

As a wholesaler, you enter a contract with a seller to get a buyer for the property. You then market the property to potential buyers then choose the most appropriate one to close the contract.

Once you start wholesaling, you will be surprised at the many benefits associated with the business. This is because you do not need formal training to engage in the business, and you will be able to make quick cash within a relatively short time.

This book details everything you need to understand before and during the wholesaling process. It highlights the difference between retail and real estate wholesaling. It also informs you of the many benefits of wholesaling, requirements of becoming a wholesaler as well as the numerous strategies you can use to get the best buyers on the market.

While at it, you will also get to know how to convince buyers to purchase your deals and how to negotiate potential deals. Moreover, the book outlines the tips you need to succeed in the business, as well as the challenges you may face along the way and how to overcome them. Basically, this book serves as a great information tool for beginners and also experts in the wholesaling business.

If you are hearing about this concept for the first time, or if you are just seeking to expand your knowledge about real estate wholesaling, then you have found the right resource for you.

Chapter 1: What Is Real Estate Wholesaling?

Generally, wholesaling means selling of merchandise or goods to a buyer, who repackages and sells them to other buyers, at a profit. The wholesaler repackages the goods and mostly sells them in smaller quantities, but still making interest on the overall purchase price. Using the same concept, this is applied to real estate.

Wholesaling in real estate is where a person becomes a middle man who matches property owners with buyers. Most of the time it is undervalued property or property which has been on the market for too long without getting buyers due to one reason or another. As a middle person, you are more involved in identifying the property, getting the details about it and letting potential buyers know about the existence of the property. You can find great real estate deals and end up making a great profit if you play the game well.

In some cases, there is the option of you by contracting to buy the property, but in most cases, the use of assignment contracts applies. This simply means, once you identify the property that you think would make a great deal, you get into a contract with the seller and then sell the contract to someone else who would like to have the property, using the agreed on terms with the seller.

Note that as an investor, you have the option of not selling the property, rather the contract you have with the seller. You do not end up making money wholesale itself, but on the contract that you sell at a fee from someone else interested in investing. This works great for most people who want to deal in wholesaling when they have no much money for investment.

How It Works

Since you will be seeking to either sell the property to investors or be an investor yourself, one has to first know how to go about the whole business idea for it to be successful. As a middle man, you would need to understand that the buyer will always want to buy property below their current market value. You would then need to find and control properties that you are sure are undervalued, as this would give you an edge.

As much as it sounds like a simple idea, real estate wholesaling is not for everyone. It needs one to commit a lot of time and to be very patient. It also requires great communication and marketing skills, as you will constantly have to talk to people and sell them your ideas. Also, having a great network of similar minded people really helps as one can make a deal from word of mouth connections. If the thought of having conversations and making negotiations makes you shudder, then this might not be for you.

On the other hand, going into this as an investor is another way of dealing. You would need to have enough knowledge of real estate so as not to get caught up in bad deals. This can be either working with realtors or doing a lot of due diligence before getting into any agreement with anyone. There are also some strategies for beginner investors:

Having a bank account for you to deposit profits: This is simple and clear but can be very difficult for any individual without some discipline. Having an account where you can make your profit savings helps one to track their growth and also save. Then do follow up transactions and keep saving so as to accumulate a good amount of money to help you get into real estate. This is something that does not come cheap; hence a lot of discipline is required.

Once the profit is sizeable, you can take it into buying property so you can become an owner. You then would have the option to either go retail or wholesale. Once you buy and hold, it is even easier to build your portfolio as it is easier to make more profit when dealing with own property than being a middle person.

Difference Between Real Estate Wholesaling and Retail

There is a great difference between these two, where one needs a lot of work input and has higher risks involved. Also, it mostly depends on the property and process involved in getting it on the market.

Retail	Wholesale
1. When buying retail, the property is always in good condition and	1. When buying in wholesale, the property is mostly dilapidated and

ready for occupancy or use. In case of any small repairs, the investor would have the seller fix them, or reduce the purchase price so that the buyer can fix them once they get the property.

2. Retail homes are always full-priced and mostly sell at or above the market prices. This is because they are mostly in a well maintained state and any fee that would be required to maintain them would have

would need a lot of major repairs. If one is lucky, it would need just some slight cleaning up. This is an exception as most wholesaling properties are always in a dilapidated state.

2. Wholesale real estate is mostly under the market value, as they would be not in the best condition. Some would even be rundown buildings, which have never been inspected or land rates not paid for a while.

been cleared. 3. They mostly have giant contracts that are highly detailed, are well inspected and mostly take weeks to close. This is because the process is highly involving and there are other people involved in ensuring that the property meets the buyers' standards. This highly protects the buyer of any losses, especially which come up later after ownership. 4. In retail, realtors are highly used,	This puts the buyer at risk, hence why they mostly go for low prices, giving the buyer room to make the changes themselves. 3. The contracts as always small, with few details which might not include inspection periods as this, is always considered in the cost. They also mostly last few days. This creates a bigger risk as one might end up buying a property that would end up costing them more in maintaining

and most of them are experts in the real estate field. These serve a useful purpose as they would help a buyer know how to negotiate, and also guide them on the real value of the property, as compared to what the broker is offering. The realtors act as middle men for the buyer, and the risks one may encounter are covered, as chances of being duped are very low.

than expected. If the values estimated are not right, then the buyer would definitely incur losses once they have owned the property and finished with the contract.

4. In wholesaling, there are no realtors and no one does the inspection for you. In the case of a beginner investor, they might make the wrong financial decisions without knowing it.

It is highly recommended that as an investor/buyer, get training when dealing with real estate wholesaling of always pay off someone to walk the journey with you. This is the only way one can avoid running into major losses or making bad investment decisions.

As a middle person in the deal, one is also advised to have a lot of background on the properties so they can make genuine deals and not short change a buyer. This also helps with reputation, especially if one is doing it as a full time job and planning on expanding their market.

Benefits/Advantages of Real Estate Wholesaling

- One can make quick money: Closing deals can be as easy and quick as possible. This works as soon as one is able to get a match for the property, and they agree to sign the contract or buy it. For this to be possible, one needs to be thorough and do a great job at the initial stages of the process. This also works best when the seller knows what the buyer wants, and gets them the right fit. It becomes easier with experience.

- Little to no initial money needed: You can have very little to no money at all and still be able to work out a deal. This is because all you need to do is get into an agreed upon contract with the seller then get the deal working. Most of the time what one would need is earnest money, which is always a very small figure.

- No need for securing finances beforehand for the deal. In most cases, one would have to invest heavily when dealing with real estate. This is easier for real estate wholesaling as one only needs to sell the contract, and not the property itself. Hence they do not need much capital.

- No ownership of the property: owning property comes with a lot of requirements: doing repairs, maintenance, etc. As a broker, one does not need to worry about this, as they are never the owners of the property.

- You do not need storage space for any inventory. This is because your inventory is mostly already existing property, hence no need for physical storage, which would amount to extra costs.

- You don't need any employees to invest in. This kind of investment just needs you as an individual, as it does not really involve a lot of human capital. Once you have done all the research on properties and got the right value, signed a contract with the seller, then you are good to go by just looking for buyers. This can be done in so many easy ways, even online. Depending on one's proactive nature, they can comfortably do it all alone.

- There is no need for insurance or employer taxes involved: dealing in real estate wholesaling does not need one to pay any insurance or taxes, as these are mostly covered on the property itself. This means the cost goes to either the buyer or the seller, depending on how well the property has been maintained. In case of any fee owned, this would be figured in the valuation of the house.

Disadvantages of Wholesaling

Just like any other venture, real estate wholesaling has its own shortcomings that anyone wanting to get in should know beforehand. This is helpful in risk preparedness and setting of expectations:

- **You have no control over the market**: The real estate world is a constantly changing one; hence one would have to work with what is always available at the time they are in the deal. There are times the value of the property would be high while other times it would be low, depending on the demand in the market and the location of the properties in question. As a seller/buyer, always make sure you are up to date with the latest trends and how other people are doing so as not to fall too short or go too high in your costing. This is why it is advisable to have wholesaling as a side hustle and not as a main job.

- **Difficulties in finding buyers**: As simple as it might look, getting buyers for real estate properties can be quite hard and need a lot of commitment and patience. Having no buyer simply means making no money; hence as a middle person, you would need to do more than marketing to make it in wholesaling. As you do more of it, you improve your clientele list and might benefit a lot from referrals.

- **Growing and keeping up potential buyers**: Different buyers always have different tastes or needs. Once you have several potential buyers, it can be very challenging to constantly know and keep up to date with their changing tastes. Some investors will want one thing today and want something different in six months. This means your strategy has to be very flexible to accommodate them, which can be quite a task.

- **No guaranteed income**: As it is clear that one cannot have control over the market and its prices, it means that you might not always make money from wholesaling. This also takes some time and expertise to be assured of making deals. Otherwise, it does take time to have a constant income from this kind of business. Also, depending on how good one is at it, it does take time to start constantly earning from wholesaling.

Is Real Estate Wholesaling for You?

So, how do you know that real estate wholesaling is meant for you? Here are a few pointers:

- You don't like the risks that are associated with traditional real estate investing. Well, traditional real estate investment methods are all about owning a piece of property then letting it sit for a while till it appreciates in value. When you are busy getting worried about what might happen in the market, other people are selling off their property and sleeping till morning without any worries.

- You don't have a lot of cash to invest. If you are just starting out and you don't have so much cash to invest, the best to do is to go for real estate wholesaling. Remember that most of us want to get into the real estate business because we don't have money and we want some. Remember that traditional investing isn't easy when you don't have money stacked away somewhere.

- You have a poor credit score. This is when you have a poor credit history and you cannot run real estate traditionally. Real estate wholesaling doesn't require you to have the right level of credit which makes it ideal for you.

- You have no experience as a real estate trader. If you are just starting out with real estate investing, then this form of trading is for you. Take time to understand how it works then you will be good to go. It represents the perfect way to get into the real estate business. Since it is risk free, you don't have any barriers between you and the success that you are after.

- You have the passion. If you have the passion to look for properties and then sell them off later on, then you are in the right place.

Chapter 2: Real Estate Wholesaling Steps and where it Works

Wholesaling can be a little complicated when starting out, but there is always a silver lining in all the hard work. When you manage to sell, you create a win for the seller and yourself. For the seller, they might be facing foreclosure and need to make a quick sale to avoid any more financial breakdowns. For you, you will be able to make some neat profit in case you do manage to get the property off the market. In some way, you also create wins for the buyer, as they can get a good deal at a low price.

Simple Step by Step Guide on How to Wholesale a Real Estate Property

Finding the Property

First of all, one needs to find the right property to get a great deal in wholesaling. Most of the best properties for contracts are always in a bad or imperfect state.

Typically, these can be abandoned rundown houses, which are up for closure due to one reason or the other. This happens a lot where such houses are auctioned to the public.

Another way to find a property is to look for one that has been on the market for some time. Most owners of such property get desperate; hence, one can get a great deal out of it.

Quick ways of identifying distressed property:

- Lawns that are uncared for

- Garbage that would be littered all over the house or compound
- Piled up documents/papers in the house
- The wall structure of the building or roofing would be old

There are many other ways to identify the property, but these would be quick clues to know that it is unoccupied.

Work on the Numbers

Once you have your properties listed, do a thorough review and work on costs for the property. While doing this, the investor has to make sure their fee is worth the contract being sold. This means you have to look at everything. By everything, I mean any needs for repairs or upgrades to go to the property.

One needs to consider a few things when doing the costing:

- Land title fee

- A fee to get the property evaluated and knows the kind of repairs it would need.
- Getting services of an appraiser

Once you have figured out the approximate cost of the above, then one can know the much they will need to put up for the deal and how much you will make off the contract. Usually, one would want their fee to be a bit higher than the cost of the property, as that is where the profit will come from.

Find the Property Owner

Once you have gone through getting the details of the property, then you would need to find the owner. This is because you would need to get into an agreement with them, as you cannot wholesale their property without their approval. When talking to them about the property, always ensure that they do know that they need you to get it to the market. A seller would need to know that they need to sell a product for them to be comfortable in letting it go. Otherwise, most would hang on to it if they do not see the need of letting it go in the first place?

Negotiate the Contract with the Owner

This is the most crucial step when wanting to get into wholesaling. You would need to negotiate a great deal so that it can be easier for you as a broker to find an investor and also make a good amount of profit from it.

This is where you will have to deal with margin. The larger the margin for the potential buyer, the higher is your fee. This means you would need to negotiate an excellent price for the property, working with the seller to ensure what you end up with will earn much more for when it gets to the potential buyer.

At this point, you can bring up any repairs or construction costs that will be input in the property. Then you get to know the current price of the property and potential price after it has gone through upgrading. Always push the seller to lower the cost, as this works to one's advantage when the property is finally sold.

While doing this and setting up the costs, always remember to cover any risk factors that you may encounter along the way. If you can have an escape clause (also called a contingency clause) in the contract, it would be great. This covers the broker in case of any eventualities like the property not passing the inspections, or if the value is not high enough, and finally if the property has issues with the land title.

· ***Contingency clause**: this is a clause that is inserted into contracts that would be helpful to both parties in case of any eventualities in the business deal. In most cases, if the party required to satisfy this clause fails to do so, the other party is automatically released from the contract obligation. These clauses also may require the buyer to obtain some financing, the property to pass some* *specific inspection or appraisals done before being put on the market.*

It is also advisable to buy enough time with the seller, so as you can have ample time to get a buyer on board on or before the negotiated closing date. When one goes beyond this date, they may end up losing all the effort up in getting the contract in the first place.

Find a Buyer

When you have everything else done and the contract signed by both parties, it would be time to look for a buyer. This doesn't have to be any buyer. However, it is advisable to scan the market and find the best fit. You can achieve this by:

· ***Joining real estate groups/clubs within that area:*** These groups are a great way of interacting with people who would be interested in real estate investing. The majority of attendees would be already aware of what they want hence joining such groups opens up opportunities for you and increases the chances of one getting buyers.

· ***Do a lot of networking at auctions/real estate sales:*** Identify any local auctions or sales which you can be attending. This is a place where one can also quickly meet potential buyers and also have a high chance of knowing the market trends and value on a property.

· ***Advertise on online forums you are aware of that attract investors:*** There are several online forums depending on one's location, where an individual can create accounts and market online. These forums also have many investors and brokers, so one has to be proactive at their digital marketing skills to make a kill. Also, ensure that the forums are genuine and are not pegged on any fraud-related matters. You can always tell by looking at the ratings over some time.

· ***Physically go round and reach out to real estate buying/selling firms***

around you: You can find out a way of working with existing firms by going for one on one meetings and stating your offer. Some firms are open to working with independent brokers at a fee; hence, this would be a positive thing for you if you got a genuine one to work with.

Once you have identified potential investors, reach out with the details and dig out their interest. Know what kind of property or deals they are most interested in and using that, know whether to give them the offer or not. Wholesaling to everyone can be draining, but once you know what the needs of different people are, it becomes much easier for you.

Mistakes People Make When Wholesaling

Not Making Thorough Effort to Understand Their Local Market

Some people go into wholesaling without understanding the local economy and what works well in different areas. This would mean they not only make wrong costings but also do not know what everyone else is doing. This is a great mistake because most investors do a lot of comparison before making a final decision on properties.

One needs to go out and look at what is happening in their neighborhood and other neighborhoods and compare, and know where they can comfortably invest their energy in.

This is a great deal in being able to stick within the market value for the property and also know how much profit/income one would end up making.

Not Knowing the Influence of the Local Government on Housing and Construction

Being in line with the government should always be a top priority for anyone wanting to get into wholesaling. This is for both the middle man and the buyer. This is because there are land rates to be paid and also taxes that come with property ownership.

Not Knowing Their Buyer Needs

As a wholesaler, you have to know the needs of your buyers for you to comfortably be able to serve them. If you do random property deals, it might be challenging to find something that will sell off as most buyers are very specific and always get fed up when a middle man does not seem to meet their needs. As you build your buyer list, always write down their objectives and needs such that you can be able to easily match them up with great deals when they come up. The more detailed you get with the buyer, the more they will trust you, and it will also be easy for you to make a sale.

Not Doing Enough Due Diligence

This simply is the math that involves the whole deal. A buyer will always want conclusive information on an agreement; such that they do not realize that some costs were left out from the contract. This means you have to ensure all kinds of charges that might come up are identified upfront for the buyer. They should get into the deal, knowing exactly what they are going to spend and how beneficial it will be for them.

This also works best for you as a dealer, because you would need to know the profit you will be making out of the wholesale. If you forget to put some clauses to safeguard the contract, something might happen, and you would end up making no profit from a sale because of not looking at details.

You would also need to be clear about the status of the property to the buyer, so they do not make discoveries when already owning the property then feel cheated. This would make one lose other potential buyers, and the real estate world is pretty small.

Not Being Open to New Trends

Real estate trends change a lot, and when involved one has to keep up with the changes. Once you become good at what you do, do not get comfortable. Instead, be more active to know what is new in the market and how it would benefit your potential buyers. When you tell a buyer there are new properties that are futuristic, they would be interested in knowing more and might even change their mind on what they want. The buyer would also feel more appreciated when they know you are investing more than your profit interests in them. You are more likely to get more buyers when they know you take their interest as a personal matter and work towards satisfying them.

In general, the start would be pretty hard on any beginner, but with a lot of practice and engaging with other investors, one can quickly make deals without going through the hustle. Also, patience is critical in this, as it might take weeks or even months for one to close a deal.

Do a lot of research and reading on wholesaling to sharpen your skills as things are always changing in property ownership.

Chapter 3: Requirements for Real Estate Wholesaling

Real estate wholesaling is a very lucrative business, but it does not work for everybody. It is a kind of investment that needs a lot of determination and commitment. It also needs adequate persuasive and communication skills since you must be able to convince customers to make a purchase. Networking skills are also essential.

Many wholesalers always struggle when starting the business. The success of the investment lies in understanding that not all wholesalers are the same. Some are good at the industry while others may struggle for a while, or not make it at all. The goal, therefore, is to avoid basing your perception of the investment on the experience of other wholesalers.

An excellent real estate wholesaler is one that has all the qualities of any real estate professional. You must be able to acquire properties and resell them at a profit. Overall, to qualify as a real estate wholesaler, you must possess most of the following qualities:

- ***High focus*** – most of the real estate wholesalers that are successful in the business are the ones who master the industry. This is the secret of becoming an expert wholesaler. Instead of engaging in all real estate niches, concentrate on one niche, and perfect your skills at it. This is always difficult to achieve as a beginner, but as time goes by, you will be able to concentrate on wholesaling as your primary business goal.

- ***Consistency*** – getting leads as a wholesaler is not easy. Therefore you must ensure the consistency of your pursuits. You must exercise your marketing skills all the time. If you get relaxed along the way, you may lose some deals with other wholesalers before they mature.

- ***Hard work*** – many people think that wholesaling can be accomplished online, at the comfort of your home or office. This is, however, not the case. If you intend to make some good income from your investment, you will need to hit the road and seek for good opportunities. There is a lot of cash that you can make from real estate wholesaling. However, you should never lie to yourself that you are going to get it with no effort.

- ***Transparency*** – be honest with any transactions that you carry out and anything that you work on. If you promise to do something, ensure that you do it. Honesty will ensure that you get deals from other investors. It is a great determinant for success in the wholesaling business. You will need to explain your current deals and the levels of risk involved to potential buyers. To maintain some level of transparency, you must also ensure that you respond to any questions others might have about your deals.

Financial Requirements for Wholesaling

One advantage of real estate wholesaling is that you do not need to have a license to trade. All you need is to purchase the property, then start planning on when and how to sell it. However, you should be conversant with the whole wholesaling process before you start.

Although obtaining a license is not a must, doing it gives you several benefits, including easy access to MLS platforms with a wide array of wholesaling opportunities. Having the license will also help you to build a strong network of fellow wholesalers as well as prospective clients.

Once you understand the business, you can then secure the right amount of cash you need to get started. Even if you locate a property that you wish to purchase, it makes no sense if you do not have enough money to complete the purchase transaction. If you do not have enough capital, you may approach a private lender for a loan. You can also get a loan from a hard money lender then pay this up later. This ensures that you seal a purchase contract of your choice before losing it to another wholesaler.

The Do's and Don'ts of Real Estate Wholesaling

When engaging in real estate wholesaling, you must understand what needs to be done and what does not need to be done. Doing or not doing certain things can make you gain more or lose more from the business.

Don'ts

1. ***Do not raise a purchase offer that does not have an inspection contingency clause***. For each contract that you draft, ensure that it has an

inspection contingency clause. The work of the phrase is to prevent loss in case the property you are interested in does not meet your expectations at inspection. The provision allows you to cancel some contracts. It also creates a platform for negotiating the price of a property in case some repairs need to be done. Any time you raise a purchase offer minus this clause, you are obligated to purchase the property despite the condition you find it in.

2. ***Do not exaggerate the amount you place on the property***. Always ensure that you quote the right prices for your properties when dealing with prospective buyers. This applies most when dealing with buyers that need to pay in cash. When you exaggerate the cost of the property and the repairs needed, you lose trust with your customers. This only means that they will not come back to you in case they need to purchase more properties. Having your numbers right

also reduces the amount of time spent on negotiations. There will be less back and forth since the buyer already has a rough estimate of the property's cost.

3. ***Do not be speculative***. For each wholesaling opportunity, take enough time to monitor or analyze the property. Get an estimate of the cost of the property as you also calculate its future value. Do not create figures out of speculation. Ensure that you carry out all the necessary calculations. If for instance, you speculate that the market will rise, and then the market declines, you will end up losing a great fortune. This aspect restricts you from making emotional investments.

4. ***Do not put your interests ahead of the benefits of other parties***. For each wholesaling transaction, three parties are involved. These are the buyer, the seller, and yourself. For example, if you get a cash buyer for a property, the

transaction will take place faster, and this is a win for the seller. Another example is when a buyer repairs the property and sells it at a good profit. This automatically translates to success for him. For each deal, you get involved in; seek to understand how it can be of benefit to everyone. This way, you will be able to retain most of your customers.

5. ***Do not have an assumption that you will make a profit all the time.*** Just like every other business, investing in real estate wholesaling will sometimes fail to yield benefits. You may submit several offers yet fail to gain a wholesaling deal at the end of the day. Do not set unrealistic expectations for the business since, in most cases, only 10 percent of the transactions will go through. If you do not take a keen note of what is involved in the process, you might end up securing zero deals by the end of the day. Ensure that you send as many

offers as possible as this will maximize the number of transactions you seal.

6. **Do not use more than two marketing channels**. To transact easily, be sure to concentrate on at most two marketing streams as you seek new investment partnerships. You may, for example, decide to carry out your deals on MLS. You may also choose to focus on email campaigns as your mode of marketing. As soon as your method of choice starts generating some income, you can automate it so that you get some free time to concentrate on other things. Start with one method and wait for it to stabilize before introducing a new one. Most real estate wholesalers focus on multiple marketing channels at the same time. This always makes growth difficult.

7. **Do not disclose that you are wholesaling**. When selling a property, it is better to indicate that you are only selling the equitable interest. Inform the

buyer that you are the key person in the transaction but not the owner of the property.

8. ***Do not send deals to buyers at random***. Some wholesalers have the habit of sharing one deal with hundreds of buyers. When this happens, you may land a deal that is not too good quickly. This means that you will lose out on the best opportunity you could have received from the agreement. You should select a few prospective cash buyers and share the deal with them. As you continue selling, list down the list of sellers as you will need to contact them in the future.

Do's

1. ***Gather enough capital before getting into wholesaling***. You must establish your finances before starting real estate wholesaling. Establish your exact income and expenses. Also, list down any loans that you have

outstanding. This will help you to estimate the precise amount you need to invest in wholesaling.

2. **List your wholesaling goals**. You must understand the main purpose of wholesaling before investing in it.

Before buying or selling a property, note down the reasons why you are carrying out the transaction then determine how best to buy or sell the property. The goal should include things like the amount of cash you wish to invest in the deal, how long you expect the process to take, and the level of risks involved in the entire process.

3. **Spend time acquiring the right information**. Carry out research on wholesaling in general and on the kind of deal you want to seal before investing your capital in it. If you decide to invest blindly, you will end up carrying out unnecessary and risky transactions. Most

wholesalers lose their money because they fail to carry out the necessary research or homework on a property before investing in it.

Concerning this, you need to be careful about deals that seem to be too good. Most of these deals often bear some hidden liabilities. For instance, if you get a property that looks great yet has been underpriced, think about some of the underlying factors that may be causing the property to be priced that way. It is not easy for a property that has excellent features to be underpriced. In most cases, there is always a negative feature that is resulting in the owner reducing the price significantly.

*4. **Analyze the neighborhood**.* It is important to research the local area where the property is situated. There are several online platforms that you can use to do this kind of research. You will get some crucial information about the location of the property in general.

Besides doing this, you also need to inspect the property in person before committing your capital to it. Online research about the property is not enough. Take a stroll around the property and within the neighborhood to see if you will get some useful information from realtors and agents within the location.

5. **Check out for overheads**. Most property sellers always list the cost price and rental income of the property without listing other expenses associated with the building. As you seek to purchase a property, ensure that you understand if there are any underlying charges such as insurance, tax, repair, management, and community fees.

You need to add these expenses to your calculations. Doing this ensures that problems do not arise in the property without your knowledge. Closely monitor each income that comes in and make sure that you pay your annual taxes to avoid any accumulation of unnecessary debt.

These dos and don'ts of wholesaling ensure that you do not neglect any important aspect of your real estate investment. Learning how to implement all of these attributes may need a lot of time. Therefore you must ensure that you keep learning about the business as you continue improving on your strategies. This will ensure that you grow to become a successful wholesaler.

Real Estate Wholesaling Goals

Every wholesaler must have goals. People keep underestimating wholesaling as a real estate investment method because of the way this technique works. However, with great goals in place, wholesaling can help you generate a large amount of cash as revenue. When you have a set of realistic goals, even just a few wholesaling deals can make exponential amounts of profit for you. Goals ensure that you close deals as quickly as possible.

Creating goals is possible only when you see wholesaling as a business, not as a hobby. Proper goals ensure that you grow your investment over time. Let us look at a simple procedure you can use to set your goals.

Month 1: when starting in wholesaling, you must get out into the market right from the first day. The goal should be identifying some neighborhoods and setting these as your target locations. You can then start looking for buyers and sellers within the set locations. You may only list a few for the first month. In summary, your goals for the first month should be:

- Getting your target neighborhoods
- Identifying at least five but not more than ten buyers
- Establishing the contacts of these buyers

Month 2: now that you already have a starting point, it is also vital that you get sellers. The second month of your business should be used to find some deals from sellers. Some of the goals in this month are:

- Choosing the target area to get sellers from
- Checking out for lists of sellers from online platforms
- Settling on a marketing technique. This can be through social media, direct email or phone calls
- Listing your marketing strategies
- Sending out offers to prospective buyers and sellers

The first year: set your income targets for the year even if you just got started. Once you have identified your target customers and marketing strategy, you can begin advertising your deals actively. Estimate the number of transactions you need to close to reach your annual target and seek better ways of getting such deals.

With these goals in place, you also need to implement a few tricks to ensure that you achieve them. Here are some of the tricks used by most wholesalers:

- ***Have the seller in mind*** – the fundamental objective of real estate wholesaling is to purchase a property from the seller at the littlest amount possible. Doing this gives you a chance to resell the property at a good profit. However, it is never easy to convince a seller to accept your price even if they are having a challenge with finances. Each time you approach a seller, you must first think about their welfare and what they will gain from your deal. If you push the prices too low, you will not get the property. How you approach the seller matters a lot when it comes to wholesaling. When you become considerate of the seller, you will seal more deals than when you put your interests and the interests of the buyer before everything else.

- ***Create a strategy for exit*** – this strategy determines when you need to close deals. You may get a property at a reasonable price, but if you delay selling it off, you may lose some amount. Every wholesaler should have a list of buyers to ensure that each property that is available for sale gets a customer. More buyers often translate to faster deals. Out of every deal you offer, there will be at least one interested buyer. Seek opportunities to network widely. Through this, you will be able to build your list accordingly. As you meet people, find out the kind of properties they are looking for. Check your list of sellers to determine if there is one with a property that meets the requirements outlined.

- ***Carry out follow-up activities*** – each opportunity you get should serve as a platform for more business in the future. Once you close a deal, spend time interacting with the parties involved so that you keep growing the relationship. Find out if they have any issue with the sealed contract and whether you can help solve the problem.

What You Are Not Told in Real Estate Wholesaling

When venturing into real estate wholesaling, there are several things that you get to learn. However, there are facts and ideas that you will not get from a real estate class. You will not be told that:

1. The investment requires a lot of capital. It is a bit expensive to become a real estate wholesaler
2. From what you learn in class, only a small percentage applies to daily investment processes. Every wholesaling experience requires different sets of skills, experiences, and strategies
3. You need a lot of patience. When it comes to real estate in general, there

is no way to succeed overnight. You need to spend a lot of time, resources and efforts to get where you want to be

4. Wholesaling is not easy. It is similar to the marketing of products since you must have the right skills to convince a buyer to purchase a property. You should improve your tactics each day as the number of clients grows. The moment you stop innovating ways of striking deals, your business starts going down

5. Your friends may not necessarily become your clients. Do not get into the business with the hope that your friends will become your number one client. You will be surprised that none of the people you get as clients are from your friends' list. Most of your customers can be total strangers.

6. You will be remorseful at times. Most buyers always feel remorseful once they have purchased a property, and this remorse may be translated to you as well. However, the more you master the business, the less emotional every transaction becomes. You must continue doing business so

long as you are not doing anything wrong

Real estate wholesaling has several significant aspects that you need to focus on if you want to make a profit from it. The business revolves around assisting people, and this is what makes it more fulfilling. If you are struggling to get buyers and sellers, you can consult a professional for assistance.

Chapter 4: Wholesaling Strategies and Profits

Real estate entails carrying out property transactions on behalf of the buyer and the seller at a profit. As a wholesaler, you benefit from the price of reselling the property without becoming the sole owner.

Wholesaling is also known as flipping. It bears several advantages over other real estate businesses. You do not need an office to operate from; neither do you need employees or insurance cover for your business.

Strategies

When it comes to real estate wholesaling, there are several strategies used to gain buyers and sellers on the market today. These strategies help you to get real estate opportunities that you can engage in to generate profit. The primary point is always to find the right deals and maximize your time on them to get something good out of them. Some of the strategies you can use to get buyers and sellers include:

- *Direct mail marketing*
- *Local marketing*
- *Networking*
- *Online marketing*

- *Driving for dollars*

Direct Mail Marketing

When you are a wholesaler, you want to get deals at a price that is below the market price. This is what enables you to make a profit. The cost must balance in a way that ensures the buyer makes some profit should he decide to resell the property. If the price of the property is set too high, the buyer might get stuck, meaning he will not be able to sell the property off.

A great way to obtain deals that are favorably priced is through the use of direct email. To use this strategy, you need to first come up with a list of your target clients then keep emailing these severally. The good thing with direct mail is that you can acquire email lists from third parties. These lists are often customized in a way that meets your wholesaling requirements. They always contain names and contacts of homeowners who are seeking to either purchase or sell off properties. You must note, however, that getting these lists will cost you some money.

When you consistently send emails to the contacts on your list, you will be able to get some leads. The content of your message matters a lot since it will determine how your target buyers respond to your requests. You must, therefore, identify a particular motivation and incorporate it into your communications. For instance, if a seller promises to give out their property then change their mind later, you may offer some discount that will keep them in the deal. This also applies to the buyer; especially when the property in question needs some repair work done after the purchase. How you follow up on your leads also determines if you will get them. The buyer or seller may fail to contact you, but if you keep refreshing your conversations with them, you might land a great deal from them.

Most buyers who have used this strategy always admit that it is one of the best ways to create a consistent flow of real estate wholesaling opportunities. Once you have categorized potential buyers and sellers in terms of location, income level, and age among other attributes, it is easy for you to know when to send them. As your business grows, the lists may also increase significantly. At this point, you may need to engage a third party individual or organization to be sending the emails on your behalf. This is what makes direct mail a bit expensive. However, the strategy remains relevant when you are making enough profit from it. For example, you may spend $2000 on the costs of sending the emails but get three deals that give you a profit of $6000.

In this strategy, you spend money to gain money. You can therefore not use it effectively if you do not have any money allocated to it. Most wholesalers have testified of closing up to 90 percent of the deals sought using this strategy. Mailers always comprise of postcards and letters. The way you design these mails determines how they are received. Always ensure that you use a promotional tone.

Networking

Another great strategy you may use to get deals for your business is by interacting with other real estate investors. You can achieve this by joining networking groups within your local area. You may also join some online networking forums where you can get information about real estate networking events within your area. As you continue to network with others, you may be lucky enough to find investors who are willing to delegate some deals to you. This can occur when the investor has too many transactions or is just too old to transact. You may also find wholesalers that are seeking to partner with others for one reason or the other. All this only creates more business for you.

Most estates always have at least one club created explicitly for real estate investors. If you want to get deals within your area quickly, you must join such clubs. These create an avenue for you to land some of the most excellent deals. As you build your credibility and reputation in such clubs, you will stand a high chance of succeeding in your business. You must always treat everyone you meet in such clubs with courtesy because you may not know who will eventually become your client.

Such clubs always comprise of sellers and buyers. As you interact with people, you will always find some buyers who are just seeking the right person to give their property to. You will also learn a lot from some of the experts within your local area. Joining such clubs may cost you a small amount of cash, but it is worth trying. Eventually, you will become the go-to wholesaler for most deals that arise within your area. Investors who have a lot of deals on their hands may approach you to assist them. Even if such agreements do not give you much in terms of profit, they can help you build your brand. Eventually, you will be able to get deals without having to market your business too much. Always remember that wholesaling is a relationship-based kind of investment. The more relationships you cultivate, the more profitable your business gets.

Local Marketing

Local marketing entails looking for deals within your local market. This is one of the cheapest real estate wholesaling strategies. You can begin by creating some visual signs and posters. You have probably seen samples of these on telephone poles and buildings within your estate. You can create these signs and add your contact number in case someone wants to reach out to you for a deal.

One great attribute that makes these signs work is where you position them. For example, you can opt to place them at a junction, next to a mall or anywhere where there is high human traffic. When used correctly, this strategy becomes more effective than direct mail campaigns. You can also decide to buy a list of FSBO properties within your area then contact their owners to get some deals within your area. Most FSBO property owners avoid using agents because of the massive commissions involved. However, if you approach them with a better deal than that of the agents, you may convince them to give you the work of selling the property on their behalf.

Online Marketing

Online platforms grant you the opportunity to reach out to millions of people within a few seconds. One such platform is social media. To use online platforms effectively, you need to set up a website where users can get more information about your wholesaling business. You can decide to set up a simple website using WordPress or a more dynamic website using more sophisticated tools.

When done creating the website, you can come up with profiles on Facebook, Instagram, Twitter, and many others, depending on your preference. Highlight your business terms and conditions on these profiles while also ensuring that you remain promotional. Make your posts on these platforms consistent. You will be able to get connections and referrals to great wholesaling opportunities. However much you desire to make a profit, ensure that you do not exaggerate your terms of business. At first, you may receive only a few or no leads, but as you continue to build your accounts, you will realize more and more opportunities coming through. Sometimes you may stay for several days or weeks without getting any deal. This should not discourage you from continuing to build your online presence.

Besides social media, you may also decide to get some deals on Craigslist. The site has a real estate section that highlights excellent wholesaling deals. One advantage of the craigslist system is that it is free to use and you can automate your deals flow with ease. It is the best alternative to direct mail marketing since you do not spend any cash on marketing your business.

Driving for Dollars

The fifth and last strategy is known as driving for dollars. This strategy is commonly used by dedicated wholesalers who are ready to go to any extent to get a wholesaling deal. The approach involves driving within your areas of interest to look for properties that indicate distress. Some of the things to look for include broken walls, windows, neglected compounds, and junk in the compound.

When you spot such a house, you can write down the exact location address then visit the relevant online platforms to find out more about the property. If you get information about the owners of the property, you contact them by mail or phone to find out if they are willing to sell the property.

Most wholesalers do not like this strategy because it involves a lot of processes.

However, when you become committed to it, you can easily land some good deals at no cost at all. The more you understand the area of interest, the easier it becomes for you to identify some properties in distress.

How to Make a Profit from Wholesaling

As a wholesaler, the amount of money you make from any deal depends on many factors. Before getting into any agreement, you need first to understand the property after repair value or ARV. You have to know how much you can sell the property once it has been fully renovated.

Determining the ARV of a property entails comparing some of its aspects with other properties. This also includes comparing the price of the property with others within the area in terms of the pricing. You can do this by identifying a few properties that share some characteristics with your potential investment, then using these to carry out the comparison. This will help you to estimate the final cost of the property once you have completed all the repairs.

Understanding that wholesalers are only matchmakers that link buyers to sellers enable you to know how much you will make from a deal before closing it. One advantage of wholesaling is that you can use several ways to gain profit. How best you negotiate an agreement with the buyer and seller determines how much you earn from it when the deal closes. Remember, as a wholesaler you only make a certain percentage as wholesaling fees although some sellers may be generous enough to share part of the profit with you.

If you do not carry out your deals right, you may spend several years working with individuals who do not sell anything. You may also find yourself wholesaling for a property no one wants to purchase. The kind of strategy you use to get deals also has a way of influencing your returns. This is because strategies like bandit signs or listing on MLS can get you instant opportunities that process quickly. Other strategies like direct mail and driving for dollars can take a while before you realize any opportunities. Delayed processing of deals translates to late income.

Another factor that influences the profit you make from wholesaling is the kind of property you get. When it comes to this kind of investment, the numbers or price usually dictates the direction of the business. You must always purchase the property at a cost that is low enough to be able to resell at a profit. The buyer only gets interested in a property whose price is attractive. This may sometimes mean that you make less profit than what you had in your initial plan. It is better to make relatively little profit from several deals than making one huge profit over a stretched period.

When it comes to analyzing the profitability of a particular house, there are several computations that you need to make. One such calculation is the 70 percent rule which states that the maximum offer you can receive for a property is 70% of its value after repair. In case you do not understand how to make these computations, you should consult a professional to do it on your behalf. In case you ignore these calculations, you will end up with wrong figures. You will stand at risk of losing some cash instead of making a profit from the property. Some deals may also take a long time to process. You must factor the aspect of time in all your computations to ensure that the property does not depreciate during the process.

The next thing you need to check out when determining your profits is the market. The kind of market you list the property impacts how long the process will take and how much you will take home as wholesaling fees. Start looking for buyers early enough. Some wholesalers postpone this until when they are about to close the deal with the seller. You need always to have a list of buyers ready even before the seller commits the property to you. As you look for deals, concurrently look for buyers as this will save you time in case the seller agrees to your deal. You can get these online or through your local investment clubs. You may also use newspaper ads and other networking events to identify potential buyers. If a property receives more than one buyer, you can decide to give priority to those buyers you have dealt with previously.

The ultimate goal of making a profit lies in building strong, lasting relationships. People that are conversant with your business tend to invest in it more than strangers. Working with people you know eases the burden of convincing them to purchase or sell properties to you. When an issue arises with the property, it becomes easier to resolve since you have already gained the trust of the parties involved. Seeking to make things easy for the investors you work with makes them wish to work with you more in the future. However, if you are the person that leaves issues unresolved, then you will lose some future wholesaling opportunities to other investors in your circle.

To better understand how much you can make from a deal, you mustn't exaggerate your profits. Increasing the actual property cost just to earn more from it may land you one or two contracts. Once buyers and sellers know of this trick, they will start avoiding your business. Remember, real estate investors always interact with one another. Spoiling your reputation with one may mean destroying it for all. Therefore you must be careful about the image you create with all the investors that you work with. Get to understand the prices on the market and ensure that you do not exceed them. If you want the business to continue working in your favor, always keep all the numbers associated with a particular deal real.

There are a few tips associated with wholesaling costs and profits. These can help you remain on course when anticipating earnings from a specific property. Let us look at some of them:

1. ***Choose a comfortable price range*** – a good number of the deals you will come across fall in the middle range when it comes to prices. Some will even have lower rates than expected. However, you always need to set a price that is favorable to you, so long as it falls within the range recommended to the buyer and seller. If you set the prices too low, you might end up getting properties that have less demand and a lot of repair issues. This will result in less or no buyer for the property.

2. ***Understand the cost of repairs*** – this is a distinctive aspect of wholesaling. Majority of the properties listed for sale feature several repair issues. You must add this cost to your final value of the property. For instance, if you do not know

how to estimate the price of the property ensure that you only get one that costs 70% or less than the market value. The lower the cost, the higher your profits

3. **Identify buyers with cash** – get a buyer who has a higher potential of purchasing the property. It does not make sense, getting a buyer who is only keen to make promises but not delivering to the contract. You must verify that the buyer is serious about purchasing the property before closing out other potential buyers.

4. **Choose the right neighborhoods** – good neighborhoods are those that feature reasonably priced properties. Lower prices may be useful for you, but in most cases, such properties do not get quick buyers. You must target some areas where other real estate wholesalers are thriving. Insecurity and several other challenges often characterize some low priced neighborhoods.

Besides these four tips, you must always look for ways to process deals faster. This is because speed and volume matter a lot when it comes to wholesaling properties for profit.

How to Wholesale with $1000

Wholesaling is one business that does not require a lot of capital to start. You may even get to sell a property with zero cash depending on your agreement with the buyer and seller. It costs nothing to learn how to wholesale. However, if you have limited resources to start, in this case, $1000, then you can do the following:

- Find discounted properties
- Get committed to one channel of business – in this case wholesaling. This will prevent you from diluting your efforts to multiple businesses

- Get a strategy that does not require money like driving for dollars or bandit signs in your neighborhood
- Start cold calling. Call real estate agents for deals on off-market properties

Chapter 5: Getting the Right Property to Sell

Now that you have got into the business of real estate wholesaling, the next vital step you need to make is to get the right property. Remember that the property you get is what will determine the amount of profit that you make at the end of it al.

While this is the simplest method for you to make much money in the real estate market, it also presents you with a challenge because you need to have the best property for wholesale. We have different tactics and levels of flipping houses this way, including the different types of properties that can be wholesaled.

As a real estate wholesaler, you have various options when you decide to sell houses on wholesale. Here are a few options to choose from.

Single Family Homes

This is most probably the most popular type of house for wholesalers. Here are a few reasons that make these houses the best for wholesale purposes:

- The prices of these houses usually appreciate faster than multi homes, and they also have a higher rental rate which means that you will attract investors much easily.

- These houses are usually cheaper than other types of units that you will opt for. They are therefore lighter on the market and ideal for people that are just getting into the rental business. They will allow you to have more disposable income that you will get to spend on other things.

- These houses are relatively easy to maintain and manage, especially when you compare them to multi-apartment buildings. Tenants that are in the houses tend to take them as their own, and this means you won't have to spend a lot of money on renovations. As a property owner, you have an easy time looking at the tenants because they aren't so many like in multifamily apartments.

- These rental properties bring in higher rental prices as opposed to every unit in a multi-unit facility. The tenants in these homes enjoy many advantages that will make them be able to pay the high amount that you ask. So, while waiting to flip the house, you can as well make some more money from them.

- These houses have a specific tenant base that isn't interested in living in apartment units. The appeal of these houses is in their privacy and the freedom to make use of the garden areas the way someone pleases. You are targeting a market segment that is the biggest – people that are after their own privacy and that need space. This means that the demand for these houses usually remains steady the whole year-round.

- These houses are easier to finance compared to other homes. This means you can get a loan for buying the home faster than you can get one for multi-apartment homes. The loans also have a lower interest rate compared to other homes.

Condos and Townhomes

The benefits of buying condos are definitely dependent on what you plan to do with the condo or the townhome. Now that you plan to sell it after a short period let us look at the various benefits that you gain when you invest in condos for wholesaling:

- Cash flow – when you buy a condo, you will enjoy some income as you look for a buyer to flip the property. The aim of buying a condo is to try and sell it off in the shortest time possible. But while you wait for this time to reach, you will benefit from the cash flow, which represents the difference between what comes in and what goes out. Additionally, the rents on condos are high, which means you will recoup a small portion of your investment as you wait for the property to sell.

- The condos appreciate in value, and this means you will be able to profit in the form of passive income. The growth in value is a good way to make more profit compared to letting the property sit and wait.

- If you hold onto the condo for some time, you will be able to pay off your loan in the shortest time possible. This is because the property will give you the income that you can use.

- While you hold onto the property, you will be able to decrease your tax obligations to a large extent. You will be able to write off a portion of your tax obligations.

- While waiting for the property to get a market, you will benefit from the passive income that comes with the entail income from tenants. With the help of a property manager, you won't have to do anything – just sit and wait for your income to grow.

- As urbanization increase, the condos and townhouses are in very high demand. This is also due to the fact that Millenials and the younger generations love the city and they are attracted to these types of homes.

- The demand for these homes is very high, which means that you will sell them off faster and make your profit more easily.

Mobile Homes

Though commonly overlooked, these homes can be as profitable as the other homes that you flip on the market. Let us look at the reasons why mobile homes are ideal for wholesaling purposes:

- Compared to single-family houses and multifamily properties, the cost of these mobile homes is lower. This means you can acquire more units at a lower cost.

- Since the mobile homeowners are responsible for the repair and maintenance of the homes, and you will not have a lot of work when it comes to renovating the home for sale.

- Since you are buying a set of units, you get to spread the risks out, and the risk for losses reduces significantly.

- With the demand for these homes hitting all new highs, the need for mobile homes has also increased in equal measure. This means that you will be able to sell off the homes faster than ever. People are now opting for more affordable housing, which means you will be able to sell the house off faster than if you had a different unit.

- Not many people have learned the secret of investing in mobile homes, which means that the competition will remain low. You won't have to fight for the available units.

Apartment Buildings

Apartment buildings are some of the top investments for real estate investors. They are usually on demand even if the economy isn't going their way. Here are a few reasons why you need to invest in apartment buildings:

- Before you sell it off, you will be able to enjoy a steady source of income. However, you need to choose the apartment in a good area and location, and you will be assured of a steady source of income.

- These types of buildings usually provide an affordable housing option that will allow people to enjoy affordable housing, something that they are all after. Apartments will always remain on-demand at all times.

- The property can easily appreciate without investing in the property at all. You don't have to invest in new carpets, windows or sidings and paint.

- These apartment buildings provide you with tax benefits. One, you will enjoy depreciation expense when you purchase the property, and you can reinvest the proceeds into a new property, and you won't pay any taxes due to the appreciation.

- The demand for multifamily houses is steady and doesn't

experience the dramatic changes that we see in office and retail.

- You have access to a host of multifamily loan products that you can choose from to finance the purchase.

Commercial Real Estate

You can also wholesale, retail malls, office buildings, and other mixed-use properties. Here are a few reasons why commercial real estate is an attractive investment for you:

- While you wait for your investments to generate interest in the market, you will be able to enjoy the cash returns that come from using the property for rental purposes.

- Commercial real estate doesn't fluctuate in the price as compared to other types of investments in the market such as stock and more.

- Commercial real estate is less

volatile compared to other types of properties. They remain valuable even when the prices rise in the market. This helps to protect you against inflation.

- The property enjoys a steady level of appreciation compared to other properties on the market.

- When you invest in real estate with the aim of flipping it, you are able to diversify your portfolio the right way.

Vacant Lots and Land

You can sell these vacant lots and land fast because many people are looking to develop their own properties the right way. Here are a few reasons why you can invest in land as a way to make some more money:

- When you have a vacant lot, you don't have to do anything on this property at all. It appreciates without investing more money in it.

- You don't have to deal with stubborn tenants, leaky roofs, burst pipes, or broken furnaces when you handle the land. Once you buy it, all you need to do is to wait for the land to appreciate.

- As a wholesaler of vacant lots, you have little competition to deal with in the first place. Everyone is investing in rental properties, but when you decide to invest in land, you are one among many other people to do this.

- When you learn to research and find the right property to sell, you will be able to buy and sell the land without having to see the land yourself. You can make the purchase and sale of the land virtually without leaving home at all.

How to Find Properties for Wholesale Real Estate Investment

Now that you know the kinds of properties that are available for you to invest in, the next step is for you to locate these properties. Remember that you need to find properties that you will sell then make a profit. Here are the top ways to get the property that will make you a hero in wholesaling.

Foreclosure Listings

For you to get the property to sell, you can explore foreclosure listings online. When you decide to go for foreclosure listings, you will be able to achieve a fast purchase, which will give you a better profit compared to others. You, however, will have to do repairs on the property. The good thing is that you will be able to know the price of the property as well as the history, which makes it easy for you to estimate what is required before you put it on the market.

When you buy a foreclosure listing, you have the ability to do all the standard inspections, including research of the title during that period.

When using a foreclosure site, you will only be able to see late-stage foreclosure, which means that you miss out on properties that are in pre-foreclosure, which is the stage where the borrower has already defaulted on the mortgage, but the bank hasn't officially performed the foreclosure.

Property Auctions

Another good place that you can get distressed properties for wholesale auctions. We have various auction sites online that you can use to get the property that you need. You can also check your local newspaper for planned auctions.

If you wish to get more options, you can go for other auction sites that are out of your target area. Many of the auction sites are always updated to give you the latest on the properties that are available.

The good thing is these sites allow you to bid on properties so that you can post the best price you need the property for. Just like other auction sites, they also have a buy it now an option for a few properties.

The competitive bidding process is fast and gives you a chance to bid on houses that you would normally fail to find at a better price. Auctions require you to put down a deposit, usually between 5 and 10 percent and then the remainder in 30-45 days that is if you win the auction.

You can opt for financing from a series of companies that offer to finance specifically for borrowers. These financiers can prequalify you in a few minutes so that you can compete with all-cash buyers.

Real estate auctions will give you a wide range of properties at different price points and will include things such as multi-family units, single homes, as well as commercial properties. Auctions can be online or in person.

These auctions happen in real-time or over a few weeks, and they usually start with a minimum price. From here, the auctioneer will allow the competitive bidder to put up a price for the property until a single person remains. When the auctioneer realizes the price, they will close the auction and then award the property to the winning bidder.

The objective and the investment timeline that you have will dictate what financing options that you have available for you. Cash is the preferred method of payment for the auction. However, you can use lenders to finance the process of paying for the property.

When you get into an auction, you need to budget for the following costs:

- Down payment of between 20-35 percent depending on the purchase price of the property as well as any other lender fees.

- Holding costs, which are monthly costs that will help, keep the property such as taxes, mortgage, and insurance.

- Repair and renovation costs, which vary according to the condition of the property as well as the area.

- Marketing costs, which is the amount that you need to spend to put the property on the market. This is usually a percentage of the property and is paid out on the sale proceeds.

Where to Find Auction listings

There are various ways to get real estate auction listings:

- ***Real Estate Auction Sites***

You can visit real estate auction sites that offer both online and physical auctions. Some of them offer both types of auctions, while others only offer a single type. You need to check out these sites and browse what they have on offer, they r requirements and more, then start looking for houses that you can bid on.

- ***Real estate Professionals***

These have a lot of information regarding upcoming auctions for real estate properties. They include brokers, real estate agents, and trustees. Bankruptcy accountants and lawyers are also good people to engage when you are looking for such opportunities.

You can find these professionals through referrals from friends, investors, and other family members. You can also decide to join a real estate investment group in the area or search for a real estate agent and ask for personal auctions.

- ***Real Estate Classifieds***

These are somewhat outdated, but you will still find listings in local newspapers. Some of the newspapers have an online presence as well, and you can get your properties on them.

Abandoned Houses

Another strategy that you can use to get the right property for wholesaling is to go for an abandoned house. An abandoned house is one that no person is living in, and the signs will tell you that the house has been abandoned for a long time. The owners will be paying annual taxes as well as mortgage payments, and so they will be interested in letting it go. You can approach the homeowner directly and make an offer to purchase the home.

If you don't have the time to move around looking for such property, you can go ahead and visit sites that list these properties in the community. These platforms have a search platform that allows you to choose the property type, kind of ownership, and attributes. Most listings come with a phone number attached.

Drive-bys

You can also locate a property for wholesale by moving around the neighborhoods in which you wish to purchase the distressed property. If you see a house that has mail accumulating with the landscaping neglected, it is highly likely that it is abandoned. The house could also belong to a child of a homeowner that is deceased or has gone into a senior facility.

However, you need to approach the home with a lot of caution, because these kids might have an attachment to the home, or they cannot agree to the terms of sale of the property. They might also be avoiding the costly repairs that come with owning such a home and will want to dispose of it. Offering to buy the property will seem to them as an attractive option that they will take up willingly.

While moving around, don't forget to contact the local people that have information on homes that are vacant. These can be mail carriers or real estate agents. Remember that real estate agents will find these homes to be a liability because their clients never want to stay near such homes.

Pre-foreclosures

These are homes where the borrower has defaulted on payment, and they have gone at least for 90 days without paying. Though the agents have in place a process that will help the owner to pay the mortgage, in most cases the property usually goes to foreclosure just because the homeowner cannot afford the amount needed to redeem them.

When you identify a property that is in this state, you get to eliminate most of the competition, and thus you stand a better chance of getting the property. You also have the advantage of negotiating directly with the lender or the borrower while you still have a lot of options on the table.

Attorneys

You will be surprised that you might find a good property from your attorney. Many attorneys run the wills of their clients, and they know when the property is to be sold or not. They also handle divorce settlements, and they know when a couple is undergoing a foreclosure at the close of the divorce, so they will know when a property is on the market or not.

Chapter 6: How to Get The Best Offer

Real estate wholesaling can be a profitable venture if you do it the right way. However, many first time investors find it a big hurdle when they realize that a lot has to go into the process. One of the major hurdles that make real estate wholesaling fail is the lack of negotiating skills.

This is understandable because for you to be a real estate wholesaler, you have to talk to sellers that are motivated to sell the property off. The seller usually seeks to get as much as they can from the deal as possible, which puts you in a corner when it comes to making sure you get the best price.

Talking to Sellers the Right Way

So, if you are finding it hard to get into the murky waters of talking to sellers, then you need to read the following tips:

Perform the Right Research

Before you can perform well in front of a seller, you need to perform due diligence about the property. First, you need to join a local investment group that will give you an idea of what is trending and what isn't. Learn to ask questions about the property that you are interested in, and sure enough, you will know what you need to do so that you can get the best deals in the area. Most of the people that are on these investment groups tend to have experience with what you are planning to do, and they will give your ideas on how to approach a seller.

The next step is for you to build a rapport with the real estate agent. At this point, ask the real estate agent to give you a list of the properties in the area and how much each of the properties goes for. This gives you an idea of what to expect in terms of price.

When armed with the right information, you will get over your fear of investing in these types of houses, because you have all it takes to face the seller.

This means you first have to know every aspect of how the wholesaling deal works, as well as knowing all information regarding the seller that you are making contact with so that you don't end up getting surprises when you are in the middle of a conversation.

It is also vital that you know what the other party wants from the deal. Dig some background information on the person so that you know whether they are having financial difficulty or are going through a divorce. Depending on the situation, you will be able to know what to say or do, especially when the negotiation isn't going your way. Remember that you have to know what the person wants so that you play with their emotions during the deal.

Practice

If you have a fear of speaking in public, you need to know that you aren't alone. It is a common aspect of negotiations. Fear usually is a result of a lack of experience that makes you fear expressing yourself in front of other people.

So, how do you go about a negotiation when you don't know how you will negotiate? Similar to any skill, you need a lot of practice in order to make things work for you. Before you meet the seller, take some time to practice in front of your friends or even the mirror. You can also take part in mock negotiations when the pressure is off.

If you have a team that you work with, try and practice the negotiations with them. This also gives them the capacity to handle negotiations when you aren't around. You can visualize a normal conversation then write down the things that you need to say, and then keep visualizing them so that you have an idea of what to expect at all times.

When you have information, and then you rehearse, you will walk into the negotiation when you are full of confidence. Confidence usually makes deals go your way.

Know What You Want, and Express It

Don't be afraid to know what you want in the negotiation. Make sure you have goals that you follow when you go to negotiation and then go for them. Achieving goals in a conversation are all about looking for a way to get what you went out for, at the price you can afford.

Don't look at the whole experience to be a confrontation at all. Instead, you need to understand that it is all a process that you have to handle the right way. Think of it as a process that is normal to you, and that you have all it takes to make it work no matter what happens. Motivated sellers are those that are out to make sure they sell the house and get what they are after – the money.

Don't look at the seller as an enemy, rather view them as someone that you need to work with so that both of you get what you want, which is a resolution to the problem at hand.

Build Rapport

People love working with other people that they like. They like working with people that are open and honest, anything contrary and the person will not work with you. Creating a rapport doesn't mean that you and the seller become very good friends, rather you need to have a certain level of respect that will cement your relationship with the home seller and give you a platform to present the message.

This means you need to focus the first few minutes of the interaction on building rapport. Ask the seller about what they do, their background, their hobbies, and interests so that you get a common playing ground. Most of the times, you will get to determine the outcome of the negotiation not by the ability to negotiate the right way, but by establishing and maintaining a rapport.

Learn

When negotiating, you are trying to tell another person about your point of view in all that is happening. You are presenting your side of the story so that the other person can give in to what you want. It is all about knowing what the other person wants from the negotiation and then finding a way to work with them.

You need to learn various aspects of the seller and the property. Here are a few things that you need to understand:

- Is the seller currently living in the property?
- For how long has the seller lived on the property?
- Is the seller the real owner, or is he selling on behalf of another person?
- When is the seller planning to move out of the property?
- Why is the seller disposing of the property?
- When is the ideal closing date for sale?
- What will the seller resort to if the property doesn't close?

These questions are hard for the seller to answer, so you need to find a way to get the responses without triggering any suspicion. What you need to tell the seller is that you have the capacity to solve their problem immediately and this is why you need as much information as you need so that you facilitate the process.

When you focus on getting the right information the best way, you will be able to get the deal at an attractive position.

How to Identify Motivated Sellers

You have heard of this term used in this section before, and you will come across it in upcoming sections as well. We need to understand what it means to be a motivated seller and how you can find one.

Without having a source for motivated sellers, you will waste a lot of time trying hard to get a deal when in reality, it won't come your way. The best idea is for you to work with sellers that are willing to sell and who are flexible in their dealings.

The challenge that many investors have known how to get these motivated sellers.

First, we need to know what it means for someone to be a motivated seller. A motivated seller refers to a person that seeks to get rid of a property that they have in their possession. A motivated seller is willing to sell what they hold at a price that is within the prevailing market range. This means that the seller is willing to sell their property at a price that is between 10 and 30 percent below the market value.

A motivated seller is also willing to sell to you the process at favorable terms, for instance, no deposit and 0 percent interest. For many people, the ideal motivated seller is the one that has all these facts in tow, but even a single one is enough to make one a motivated seller.

Motivated sellers make it easy for you to get the property on time because they are clear with what they want and how they want it. They know that they have to talk to you favorably for them to resolve an issue that they have, which is disposing of the house.

So, how do you find a motivated seller for a property that you want to sell? Here are a few pointers:

Come up with a List

You need to come up with a list of motivated sellers that you can work with at any time. You don't need to have so many people for you to make it in real estate wholesaling, start with a few, such as two and then build on the list. The list needs to include attorneys. Absentee owners, realtors, landlords, homeowners, foreclosures and many more that you can add to your list.

You can come up with your own list, but this will take a lot of time and effort. What you need to do in this case is to find a company that specializes in making lists and then have a targeted list that you can use. Make sure that you filter everything so that you get the right form of property for you. Common filters include property size and zip code.

Have a Marketing Page

Once you have a list, you need to come up with a marketing page that will attract other sellers that have something to offer. You also need a direct mail piece that you will send motivated sellers that have something to offer. Additionally, you need a webpage that will give your contacts. Motivated sellers will use the page to contact you or to share their contact info with you.

Send Your Mail

Once you have a list of motivated sellers that are willing to handle your business, you need to introduce your self-using direct mail. This is the first contact with the sellers that will tell them that you exist and that you are ready to do business with them.

A single mail won't do the trick; you need to send out several emails in order for you to get the right response from the seller. Make sure the marketing message is convincing and compelling enough to make the seller want to give your business.

Remember that the response rate is usually about 5 percent, so know that if you sent 100 emails, you are looking at five responses.

Try and make the message as personalized as possible. Look at what the seller is looking for then create a message depending on their goals. This means that even if you are going to send 100 emails, you need to make sure each mail is customized to the needs of the seller.

Once you get a few leads, you need to follow them out the right way. Tell them what you need and then let them know your budget.

Negotiating Tips for Wholesale Real Estate

You need to be a good negotiator for you to strike the best deals. You will to really negotiate so that you get a good deal and then get profit from the deal.

Create a Win-Win Situation

The best negotiators know that they have to create a situation where both the seller and the buyer will win. Just because you are trying to close a deal doesn't mean that the seller doesn't know what to do. When you are negotiating, don't do it just for any small issue, rather look at the bigger picture. The costs that you see to be small might be big for the seller.

Successful sellers don't negotiate over small costs – they have a lot of topics that are ready to go in their queues. This way, they make sure everyone gets what they want at the end of it all.

Compromise

You might be hard up with what the seller is suggesting, but when it comes to making a deal, you need to learn to compromise. When looking at the contract, seek out the areas that you are willing to knock off the contract so that you end up with a quicker purchase. You might be willing to add a few thousand to the buying price so that you don't lose out on a lucrative deal.

Be Ready to Walk Away

The biggest skill set is getting to know when to let a deal go. You don't have to get things going your way each time – at times you have to let them go. Even if the property is all you have been dreaming about the whole time, it is a bad idea to try and negotiate with all the cards on the table.

No matter how good the deal is, try and maintain your focus when you enter a negotiation. Show the seller that you are ready to walk away at any time you feel like especially when you don't get what you wanted.

One of the best ways to avoid losing your footing before the seller is to make sure you still have a few properties that are lined up for you to choose from. If you really want to be confident in all you do, then have the courage to walk away. When you find that the seller is adamant not to agree with your conditions, then you need to move on to the next property that you have in your list. While the other properties might not be as good as the one you had chosen, they are crucial to act as backup plans.

Be Direct

The best negotiators on the market will be direct and decisive. The statements you make needs you to be direct and show assurance and confidence. You also need to anticipate other perspectives from the seller. Try and write a few things down that will make the deal go forward, and then incorporate affirmative language in the negotiations.

Do the Negotiation in Person

When you desire to get the best deal, it is always good to do this yourself. A face to face negotiation will make sure that everyone is on the same page in whatever the two of you do. If you cannot meet face to face, it is better to speak over the phone. When you talk face to face, you will get to learn the body language of the seller and the reactions from them. The phone cannot be a substitute for face to face interaction, but it allows you to read the tone of the person.

When given a choice between email and the phone, go for the phone because it makes for a better conversation and negotiation. You also need to remember that negotiation doesn't need to be completed in a single conversation; you can continue it later on in separate meetings according to the need to do so.

Be a Good Listener

The worst-case scenario in any negotiation is for one of the persons to lose their temper and storm out of the room and out of the deal. This puts an end to the deal and also becomes harmful to the reputation of the investor. It also hurts future deals that might come your way as well. Make sure you have your ego in check when entering the deal and be a good listener before you can react to some statements.

Once you listen and understand, you will be confident and speak well in the negotiations. However, this doesn't always go for all the people in the negotiation.

When you have a chance to respond, do it honestly and in a way that the other party will understand. Additionally, allow other people to respond to statements fully before you can counter them.

Real Estate Negotiation Pressure Points

These are those areas that you can focus on so that you can control the deal. Here are a few pressure points that you need to be aware of:

Time

Under pressure of time, many sellers become flexible, and they are willing to sell. The pressure makes the seller motivated to sell fast, for any reason and you will be able to get the deal that you want, even better. Some of the time pressure points include when a property is near foreclosure, relocating to a new station, probate and more.

Knowledge

In any negotiation, the side that has more information is always more successful compared to the side that doesn't have information. The more information you have about a seller or the property, the higher the chances that you will clinch the deal. This is why we talked about research earlier on when you are looking for a seller. Armed with this information, you have the ability to sway the decision towards you. The information you need can come from various sources, so make sure you get the right information when you are negotiating.

Options

The person that has a few options to explore will always have the upper hand in the negotiation. This is because when you have options, you get the ability to walk away at any time you feel like.

Chapter 7: Working with Third-parties

The Role of a Title Company

Title companies have several roles in real estate transactions. The title company, in this case, acts as a combined agent for the seller, buyer, an insurance company, and any other party that is related to the transaction at hand, such as lenders. Let us look at these title companies and what they do for you:

Title Search and Review

These companies have access to a lot of information, and they will help to search and review any titles for a property that you might be interested in. the title companies provide you with information on the status and the condition of the property.

The company will give you the information that you can use to make decisions. You get the information in the form of a title report or commitment for the title insurance. The company will give you information related to legal information as well as information on foreclosures.

A title search will confirm who the owner of the company is and will find out if there is any information that might make the process harder for you.

So, how does the title company determine that the title is valid? Well, the title company will try and make sure the property title is legitimate and such that the seller is the rightful owner of the property. There have been a lot of issues regarding the purchase and sale of properties that you cannot just jump into a deal without knowing that the property is valid.

A title search is a thorough examination of the property records to make sure that the company or the person that claims to own the property actually does. The search also makes sure that no one else can claim ownership of the property.

During the title search, the company also looks at whether the property has any warnings on it or outstanding liens, mortgages, and judgments or unpaid taxes. These pending payments usually affect the ownership of the property.

The title company might also undertake a property survey that will determine the boundaries of the plot on which the home sits on. They tell you whether there are any encroachments on the property by the neighboring plots and any easements that might impact on the claim to ownership.

Before the title company issues the insurance, they will prepare an abstract of the title showing a summary of the information that was found during the search for the title.

After this, the title company issues the title opinion letter, which is a legal document which speaks to how valid the title is.

Work as a Closing Agent

Title companies usually work as closing agents for real estate deals. This means that the title company will work as an agent of the party to the transaction. As an agent, the company will be the one to obtain signatories on the documents that are involved in closing the deal. The company then receives and then distributes the payments that are related to the transaction.

After the parties have signed all the documents, they record documents that need to be recorded, for instance, deeds and mortgages. They will make sure this works for everyone that is involved in the transaction.

Work as Escrow

Many people have had it rough with dealers that are fraudsters. When you deposit your money with an agent that you don't know, many times, you end up being scammed. The best thing for you to do in this case is to work with an escrow agent that will hold the money as part of the transaction and then they will hold onto the money till the deal is done.

For instance, the seller of the property will give the title company a title deed that shows information of the property, and then the purchaser will give the title company the down payment for the property as agreed upon. The escrow company will act as the escrow officer and will only release the title deed upon the written instructions of the seller and the buyer.

Issue Insurance Policies

Once the company shows that the title is valid, it will issue a title insurance policy, that protects the lenders or owners against legal fees or claims that might arise from disputes about the ownership of the property.

When you buy a property, you will choose from two types of insurance – owner's title insurance, which you buy to protect the owner from issues that have to deal with the title. The other one is title insurance, which protects mortgage companies. The home buyer pays for the lender's title insurance at the time of closing of the house.

Choosing a Title Company

Getting a title company is a process that you need to follow to the latter. The right company will make sure you get the right documents within the specified time. You can talk to the real estate agent, or peers that have recently bought a home and they used the same process. When you get the recommendations, try to research about the companies so that you understand everything about them.

Get a title company that has enough experience doing the things that they are supposed to do. You can contact the better business bureau to check whether the company has any complaints coming in from previous customers against it.

When you are looking for premiums for insurance, make sure you shop around so that you get the best one that will allow you to enjoy the benefits of buying a property. The premium should have as little exclusions as possible and should cover the full price of the home.

You also need to look at the convenience of the whole setup. The good thing is that these days nearly everything is done online, though at times you need more than this. Most of the companies will be able to locate exactly where you live and will send over someone to meet with you personally any time you need to do something.

Experience is necessary. The number of years which the company has been operating won't tell you everything, but at least it will tell you how credible the company is so that it stays relevant all the years. This shouldn't mean that a newer company can't do the job, but it will need some testimonials for you to trust them to the extent that you give them business.

You also need to look at their reputation. For reputation, try and look for information online. Additionally, a company that is reputable will give you references when you request them.

The company you hire needs to offer a wide range of services that you need. While some transactions need to be detailed than others, it is vital that the company you pick can handle all the ones that you desire.

No matter how reputable or how recent a company is, or how big the transaction that you are making is, you need to use agents that are able to answer all your questions so that you will be able to make informed decisions at all times. Most importantly, you need to feel like your business matters to everyone. The title company needs to be responsive to your needs and will be available all day.

The title company needs to have an in house attorney at hand for all transactions. Remember that there aren't any two transactions that are alike and issues might arise that will require an attorney. Having an attorney is also a plus because you will get direction instead of something happens. The attorney will also make sure that you are protected and there aren't any delays in the transaction.

The company that you choose needs to subscribe to industry best practices. You need to look at the website of the company for their history and involvement with the local industry the right way.

The company you choose needs to be responsible and trustworthy; this is because they are coordinating one of the biggest purchases of your life, and there shouldn't be a mistake at all. If the company lacks solid processes and technology in place to avoid the mistakes that come with handling your work, then you might have delayed closing. Worse, the purchase might not go as intended, and this will impact the legal rights you have to the property.

How Much Do You Pay?

The cost of the title insurance will depend on the size of the loan and will vary greatly depending on the state of the property. The good news is that the premium that you pay is a one-time fee that you only pay at closing; it isn't an ongoing expense. You can decide to ask for a discount on the title insurance depending on the rapport you create with the company.

Pre-purchase Inspection

This might seem like one of the most tedious aspects of purchasing a property, but without a building inspection, you will be going into the deal blindly, and you might end up losing out on what you have taken time to purchase.

A real estate inspection is like a test drive, and it will let you know whether the property that you are thinking of buying is worth the price that the seller is asking or not. It also tells you whether the property is worth buying or it isn't.

When you use the home inspection before you get home, you will be able to shine a light on the shortcomings of the property and get to save yourself thousands of dollars. Inspections also keep your tenants safe at all times. Sadly, you will find that many buyers tend to avoid the home inspection step when they decide to buy the home. They do this with the main aim of saving a few dollars that don't mean too much, and thy end up realizing later on that an inspection would have been a godsend.

What is a Pre-purchase Inspection?

This is a process whereby a qualified inspector assesses the condition of the building. The inspection is supposed to cover anything and everything ranging from cracked walls to faulty roofs. The aim of the inspection is to come up with a report that shows the extent of the faults and whether they can be repaired or not. It also shows how much the repairs cost.

Many buyers will ask the inspector to check for pest damage during the inspection process, but this might cost you a little extra, but this might cost a little extra.

The Components of a Pre-purchase Home Inspection

Purchasing a property is such a huge decision that you need to make, and you cannot be over-informed when it comes to making the final decision.

Let us look at the four components that make a pre-purchase home inspection successful:

Water

One of the biggest components on an inspector's checklist is water. Water damage might make a client refuse a property. The inspector checks for leaks around the house and makes sure the plumbing system is in the right shape. The inspection also looks for signs of mold that might be a huge turn off for any prospective client.

The Structure

If the foundation of a building is sound, then it will be in great shape for several years. This is an advantage to the owner because they will have the assurance that the house will last longer for them without structural repairs. Many of the structural and foundational issues can be handled, but others cannot be repaired, which makes it hard for you. Make sure you know exactly what is needed so that you don't spend a lot of money on the repairs, which might eat into your profits.

Electrical System

The inspector will look over anything that can be turned on and off. It is vital that the electrical system in the home works perfectly because you need appliances to work the right way when the client moves in. Older homes usually have an issue with their electrical systems, and since the building codes have changed over the years, most of the older homes haven't changed so much.

Myths about Pre-purchase Home Inspections

Let us look at a few misconceptions that make home inspection doubtful for many people:

Inspection is for Termites Only

Home inspectors look at so many things ranging from the interior to the exterior. The aim is to make sure that the home is ideal for purchasing and it is habitable. It is also a way to show that the price that has been set for the property is worth it.

You Shouldn't Be There during the Process

Some people have gone around saying that you shouldn't attend the inspection because it will disturb the inspector and he won't do a good job. Well, the inspectors appreciate it when you are there with them, and you can point out a few issues that might disturb you. They take this chance to confirm or change the way you think about many things. When you attend the inspection, you will be able to do away with any fears that you have at the moment.

You need to understand that at times written reports don't tell you what you will expect fully. If you are out of town and you cannot attend the inspection, you can hold a conference call so that the inspector can clarify a few things about the report.

The seller Is Responsible for Fixing everything

Many people feel that the seller is the one that is responsible for fixing everything that is wrong with the house. This is a wrong myth, because usually repairs, which are usually serious, need to be negotiated. If the inspector discovers serious issues that need to be handled, the seller can decide to back out of a deal in case they don't agree.

The Inspection is Final

Well, it might be that the inspection will identify a few areas that need to be rectified. The home inspection can be good, but it cannot be perfect. You will still find areas that need some improvement that is not on the list that has been submitted by the inspector. The home appraisal is usually based on various factors, and usually, the inspector doesn't look at the things that are working perfectly.

It Takes a Few Minutes

The best home inspection will take several hours. The time it takes to do a home inspection will depend on the size as well as the complexity of the property in question.

These myths usually make it hard for people to decide whether they need a home inspection or not. Make sure you understand every aspect of a home inspection before you make a decision.

Reasons Why You Need to Hire a Professional for Home Inspection

When buying a property, most of the people tend to perform a home inspection by themselves so that they can avoid the cost of home inspection. They believe that since they have experience buying homes, they will definitely know what to look for at any time. Wrong.

Well, as much as you have decided on what you want in the home, you shouldn't be sure that you will get what you want when you look at it. The inspector uses a set of tools and techniques to understand what the home is all about. When it is time to assess whether the home is functional, livable, and safe, it is best to give the professional inspector something to work on.

Let us look at the advantages of working with a home inspector that is duly trained to handle all the needs of home inspections:

They are Highly Trained

Experts have the uncanny capacity to perform home inspections because they have undergone training for it. They aren't just good at looking at the walls and the ceilings and floors, but they are also aware of the building codes that you need to follow in the particular locality.

They will be able to tell whether the building is violating any rules or it is good to go, and it might later come up as an extra cost to the buyer. They are also looking at the property from the perspective of making sure the family is safe.

When you are looking at a property, the emotional aspect also kicks in, and you might find yourself overlooking a host of issues that you need to focus on when making a decision. An inspector that is certified will give you their unbiased opinion about the state of the building, and they won't use emotions to make their judgment.

Remember it isn't their job for them to sell you the property; rather, they just try to make sure you have a home that works perfectly. They are also trained on how to do their job in a systematic way so that they don't leave any stone unturned. The findings are presented in a way that is detailed and easy for you to understand. The inspector will also answer any questions that you throw at them, with the aim of making sure you understand everything that is happening.

However, there is a small catch – not all the inspectors that come your way will be professionally qualified. Some of them will have a staff that is working illegally, which means you need to take time to understand what they are doing and have a background report before you work with them. Make sure that you ask for their credentials, licenses, and certifications. Conform to the association of home inspectors within the region to see if they are legit or not.

It Saves You Money and Effort

It takes a lot of money and time for you to run a home inspection the right way. This is nothing compared to the major repairs or renovations that you will moss out if you decide to do the inspection on your own. Will you climb in the attic or crawl under the home to look for cracks in the foundation? And when you get the chance to get there, do you know what you are going to look for?

When you do this, you will spend just less than 1 percent of the cost of the purchasing price of most homes. When you hire professionals, you will be able to avoid the headache that comes with blaming yourself for things that you would have avoided if you had followed the right advice.

When you work with a professional, you will get to move forward with the process of buying the property knowing too well that you are making the right decision.

Bonus Features

When you work with a home inspection company, you will get more than a simple home inspection. They will offer you complimentary services that will make you make your decision better.

For instance, they can decide to cover the repair of a certain part of the home for you for free after the inspection is done. This will reduce the cost of repair in the home and will make you sell the house faster. Others will give you a specified period that you will access their services for free, and they indicate this in their report.

Just the way there are doctors that aren't trusted, not all the inspectors are to be trusted. It is good to know the red flags that show that the person isn't to be trusted.

Signs that You Hired the Wrong Home Inspector

It isn't a must that you hire a home inspector when purchasing a property for resale, but it might turn out to be the best idea ever. There are times; however, when you hire a home inspector and things still don't go your way. You might have heard complaints from other people that they had it rough with the home inspectors that they chose to work with.

Let us look at the different ways to identify when the inspector isn't what they seem to be:

They Want to Inspect Solo

You might be for the idea that the inspector needs to do his work as you do other things that relate to the job at hand. If this is the case, then it is true, but if you realize that the inspector doesn't want you around totally, you need to smell a rat and think twice.

Many home inspectors will be able to point the issues out to you, tell you that spots are ok and need some future repair, or tell you that something isn't working at all and needs to be replaced. Make sure the inspector gives you information that is vital to the renovation of the home. A few will tell you how the home needs repairs but won't point the repairs out - run.

Not Licensed by the State

The first thing you need to ask the inspector is to show you their license that makes them work in the state. Each state has different requirements for their inspectors, and this needs to be echoed across the board. Make sure the inspector is dully licensed and will be able to work without having to look around him suspiciously.

If the inspector is not licensed to work in the state, the inspection might not be considered valid.

The Information They Have is Confusing

You might be familiar with most of the information that the inspector offers, but at least it should make sense. If the report that you receive from the inspector doesn't make any sense to you and it is in the form of a few scribbles, then you are in for a rude shock, maybe the inspector doesn't even know what is happening.

When you get an inspector that gives you information that doesn't add up, you need to try and find another person to give you a second opinion of the same.

You need to know that building codes in each state change each year, and you need to know that the old homes aren't within the code.

The Inspector Says All is Ok

This can be a red flag for you. If the inspector is telling you that everything about the property is working fine, you need to be suspicious. You might have failed to ask all the relevant questions that will make the inspector tell you what they need to find out, which is why it is vital to ask as many questions as possible.

They Delay to Submit the Report

If you find that the inspector isn't giving you the information you need until you force them to do so, you need to smell a rat. Make sure you have the information sent to you whenever you need it. If you realize that a certain section is missing, you need to be aware of the disparity and then make sure you get it.

If some of the information is missing, you need to be wary of this, make sure you consult with another buyer so that you understand what needs to be included in the inspection report, and then crosscheck when the report is submitted. If any part if incomplete or missing, you need to ask the inspector what is happening.

The report needs to be detailed and give recommendations on what to happen when the inspection is over. If the inspector submits the information that is scanty, try and avoid them.

They Don't Know What to do

If you get an inspector that is constantly asking you about what to do or not to do, you need to be very wary of them. The inspector needs to be sure of what they do in a stepwise manner. If they don't and you are with them, you need to try and look into their past.

Chapter 8: Renovating the Property

When it comes to making the property ready for the market, you need to up your game. Remember that when the home is well looked after, it becomes better for you and you will get the right price for the home.

So, once you have the property and the inspector has given you the home inspection report, it is time to act.

Signs the Property Needs Renovating

Before you can start renovating, you need to be sure the home needs renovation. Here are a few signs that the house needs renovation:

The Roof Starts Crumbling

The hardest part of inspecting the home is to check for issues with roofing. The roof is one of the features of the house that makes the client want to buy the house. If you have a house that has a leaky roof, rest assured that you will have it hard when it comes to selling it off.

The first sign that the house you have bought needs renovation is a roof that is leaking or crumbling. Remember a leaky roof also tells you that the interior of the home is not in good shape. You need to take fast action when your house has a roof that is leaky.

There are various reasons why the roof might be damaged – first, the work might have been substandard, or the roofing system has taken a beating over the years, and it has deteriorated. When the roof has undergone a lot of weather beating, you need to be ready to either install a new one or replace a few shingles.

There are many signs that will tell you the roof needs replacement or repair. Make sure you talk to your contractor so that you understand which option is feasible.

Flooring is Dilapidated

The floor takes a lot of beating from the traffic that comes into the house all the time. The state of the floor material is a good indication of the condition of the house, and when you see the floor materials coming off, you need to start renovating.

The first signs of floor destruction come in the bathroom and the kitchen. Make sure you look for cracks, fading, and dents in the flooring material. Since the bathroom and the kitchen are some of the top deal breakers when selling the house, you need to try and fix them immediately.

Renovating the floor gives you the chance to change the way the interior of the home looks like so that it can match with the needs of a client or the existing décor. When changing the flooring of the property, you need to take several things into consideration:

- The floors on the lower levels of the house are usually more exposed to moisture compared to the floors that are at higher levels. Choose materials that will be resistant to moisture such as tile, vinyl, and the like.

- Rooms that are mostly occupied in the home need to have flooring that will withstand constant traffic from the people.

- You need to avoid using carpet and wood flooring material if the property is in areas with extreme temperatures.

The Paint is Worn out

Just the way new clothes make you look younger, a fresh coat of paint will make the wall look new and clean. So, try and invest in good quality paint so that you give your walls a fresh look all the time.

The paint gets worn out due to the constant exposure to external factors such as chemicals, dirt, and sunlight. The paint starts to fade and then peels off, and the house looks aged all the time. Well, don't wait for the paint to start wearing off before you do something. Try and repaint the walls early enough so that you reduce the need for painting with a color that the buyer wants later on.

Termite Infestation

When the house starts harboring pests such as termites, you need to act immediately so that the inspector looks at the areas that need to be taken care of. Termites tell you that the materials that were used in the property were of substandard quality and you need to rectify the situation. The infestation also shows that the house is becoming very untidy.

It Is Too Small

The time is ripe for renovating if the property that you have bought is too small for the liking of a particular client. However, you need to agree with the client regarding the cost-sharing factor when it comes to adding an extension to the property. How much is more space needed? Does changing the layout benefits the client over time? How much is the client willing to put in to make sure the property suits his needs?

When the property is too small, try to make sure the options are spelled out to the client. The client might be asked to take another property somewhere else, or they might decide to forego so that you sell l it as it is. If the client is willing to take up the property the way it is, then they can foot the cost of repair.

When adding more space to a property, you need to seek the advice of an architect, especially if you don't have an idea of expanding the home without creating an additional set of rooms. It the property comes with extra space to do this, then the better.

The Home is Out of Style

Many clients are looking for a home that appeals to a wide number of people. If you have bought a property and it is out of style, you will have to struggle just to sell it. This is why you need to renovate a few items before you put it up for sale.

Well, it will be impractical to perform a total overhaul of the home and spend a lot of money only to find that the client won't pay the asking price. What you need to do is to change a few simple items and then let the rest be done by the client.

Benefits of Renovating the Property

So, even though you are planning to sell and you desire to get more money from the property, you also need to understand that renovation isn't all about getting a better price. Let us look at the benefits of renovating a home for resale.

Saves Money

Renovation gives you the chance to get more money from the sale of the property. You will attract clients faster than when you don't renovate the property, saving you the efforts of advertising and looking for clients all over the region.

Additionally, the renovation will give you a chance to save on utility bills that might accrue when you are waiting for the clients to come knocking. Remember that one of the most expensive utilities that you have to work with is energy. Making sure the house is energy efficient will go a long way to reduce the holding costs of the property.

Becomes More Attractive to Buyers

Many people are looking for a property that they can live comfortably within. There is a huge difference between a livable and comfortable home. So, a home can be comfortable but not livable at all. So, when you renovate, you are making the home to be more attractive to the buyer.

One of the things that you make possible is a better curb appeal. What do people see when they pass on the road next to the property? Is the property attractive to a person that is passing along the road? When you improve the external look of the home, you will be able to make it better, and it will attract a lot of people who will come to view it. These turn out to be possible leads for you.

When a client comes into the home, they need to feel the comfort that they are looking for. This is why the home needs to look comfortable and inhabitable. Some homes have been lived in for so long that they aren't inhabitable anymore. Many clients are looking at the house in the form of how safe their kids will be and their property as well.

Increases the Value of the Home

You are looking to get maximum return on investment when you sell the property that you have purchased. Due to this, try and make sure that you make the home more valuable. There are a few renovations that you will make that are simple, but that will make the property way more valuable to the client. When a home is more valuable, it returns more on investment than before.

Remember that the real estate industry is very competitive, and when you make the property way much valuable, you will attract clients faster than other sellers.

If the home isn't attractive, it takes a lot of time to sell as well. Many home buyers usually look at the house that they are buying whether it has been renovated or not before they make a decision to purchase.

Financing Property Renovations: What You Need to Know

When you purchase a property, you need to renovate it the right way, knowing that the investment will bring back some money. However, when you have various properties that you need to renovate, you might find yourself stuck in a rut because you might not manage to pay for everything. This is the reason why you need to have options when it comes to financing your renovations.

Let us look at the most common options you have for financing your renovation:

Self-Financing

This is ideal for smaller renovation projects. If you have a project that doesn't need something major, then you can pay as you go plan.

Credit Cards

When you have larger expenses, you will get to charge them on the credit card. However, it is not such a good option. This is because credit card debt comes with higher interest rates which means that instead of making it work for you, it might end up adding to the cost of the overall project. Additionally, the debts can be a hindrance to your credit score since they will have unexpected costs attached.

Lines of Credit

The interest that is charged on the line of credit is lower than the one that is charged on credit cards. It is also higher than the cost of interest on home equity loans. The only downside is that for personal loans, you have to repay them for you to apply for another loan.

Home Equity Loans

These loans allow you to utilize the equity in the property. You can use them to fund the major renovations such as replacement of the roof. However, this might not be feasible for someone that is planning to sell the house fast because it takes some time for you to get approved for the loan.

Cost of Home Renovation

The costs of property renovation most times go overboard because you aren't careful. Now that we have seen how to get the funding for home renovation, the next step is for you to understand the various reasons why home renovation costs tend to go overboard.

Equipment Costs

If you are looking at a renovation that needs the contractor to use complicated equipment, then you need to be ready for higher costs. Remember that many of the equipment that you will get to use isn't readily available, which makes them expensive to acquire. This increases the total costs of renovating the property.

Some of the equipment that isn't easy to find are excavators. The availability of excavation equipment is limited, and additionally, the materials that are excavated will be taken over a long distance. These factors combine to make it hard for you to make a renovation cheap.

Structural Modifications

When you decide to remodel a property, you need to make structural modifications to the external and internal structures of the home. The modifications will change the way the home handles loads. These increase the total cost of the process.

Deadlines

When you need a property to be ready in such a small time frame, you will push it hard so that you can get it done in the shortest time possible. When the work is underway, the seller might find that there are issues that arise due to the speed of handling the process. This will lead to cost and time overruns, which in turn increases the costs.

Protecting Neighboring Structures

Constructing mechanisms that safeguard other structures from damage needs you to have more materials for the task. These tasks require you to have more money which in turn increases the cost of the renovation project.

Property Renovation Mistakes To Avoid

Now that you have done your groundwork and you see the need to handle the renovations, it is time to look at the common mistakes that we have identified in home renovations. Let us look at a few:

Unrealistic Plans

When you buy a property for resale, you need to have a budget that spells out how much you will spend on each section. Even if you are working with a professional, you need to consider the time as well as the effort that you have to put into the renovation. Make sure you have in mind an idea of how the process runs so that you know what to expect. Many sellers go into the renovation process without understanding what to expect and how to get to the point.

When renovating the property, you need to be aware that other people might be living there, and you need to know how the renovation will affect them. So, make sure you plan the renovations the right way and be realistic about how much money you can put in the project.

Going Cheap

Nothing comes easy, and you need to be able to consider the budget of the whole process before you begin renovating. You also need to look at the time and effort that you put into the renovation at all times. Well, many people don't look at the cost of everything, and they will opt for the cheap stuff when it comes to purchasing the products that they need for renovation. When looking for the right products, you need to know that the prices for items vary from one season to another. They also vary in price according to the quality. The higher the quality of materials, the better the durability but, the higher the cost.

Make sure you buy the best materials for your needs and then get the right materials for the job; otherwise, you will face a lot of problems with the renovations in the future.

Hiring Wrong Contractors

You will need to hire contractors if you need the work to be done fast and in a professional way. Even though you are handy with your tools, you still need the expertise of various contractors who will help work on electrical installations, heating, plumbing, and many other systems in the property.

Before you get a contractor, make sure you vet them the right way. As much as you want to work with a contractor that is affordable, try as much as you can to get the right one to work with. The contractor needs to be experienced and trustworthy.

Failure to Get the Right Permits

Depending on where you stay and where you have bought the property, you will need to have some permits that show that the building is livable. So, make sure that you understand the laws of the state that apply to real estate and then arm yourself with the proper permits. If you fail to have the right permits, you will have a huge problem selling the property when the time comes. Additionally, you need to make sure that the renovations are done according to the regulations in the area.

Choosing a Contractor

When you decide to renovate the home, you need to make sure you work with a contractor. Here are a few tips to help you choose the right contractor for the job:

Use Testimonials

The best way to get the right contractor s to seek the advice of close people to you. Try and get recommendations from friends, relatives, and neighbors. When asking them, make sure you tell them what you are looking for and the kind of project that you are handling. You can also seek advice from your real estate agent.

Have a Bid

The best way to get the right contractor is to make them bid for the project that you are putting on offer.

The bidding procedure makes sure that you get an efficient contractor that knows what you want in advance and helps you achieve it. In the bid, make sure you chose at least three contractors that you will evaluate face to face. When you meet with the contractors, you need to ask them a few questions that will gauge their ability to work on the project.

Confirm the Information

Once you have the three contractors singled out, the next step is for you to verify the information from the contractor. Remember that as much as contractors are many, there are some that are dubious and won't give you what you need. This is why you need to inquire about them to every minute detail. Ask about their job location as well as the clientele, and then ask for testimonials regarding their past so that you have an idea of the kind of work to expect. Look at the various complaints and the positives of every contractor before you can choose the right one.

Remember that the slightest mistake when selecting the renovation expert for the task can lead to disastrous results. Make sure that you choose the best contractor using the tips that we have outlined here.

Chapter 9: Finding the Right Buyer

When you have the property ready, the next step is for you to sell it off to the best buyer. How do you get a buyer?

Before we look at how to get the best buyer for the property, you need to look at the different types of buyers that you will come across.

The Types of Property Buyers You will encounter

When selling a home, you will come across so many buyers that will make it hard for you to know which is which. Let us look at the different types and what they offer:

All-cash Show-off

This type of buyer will be cocky because they feel they can close a deal in a matter of minutes. They know that they have the financial muscle to go for a short escrow period to buy the house.

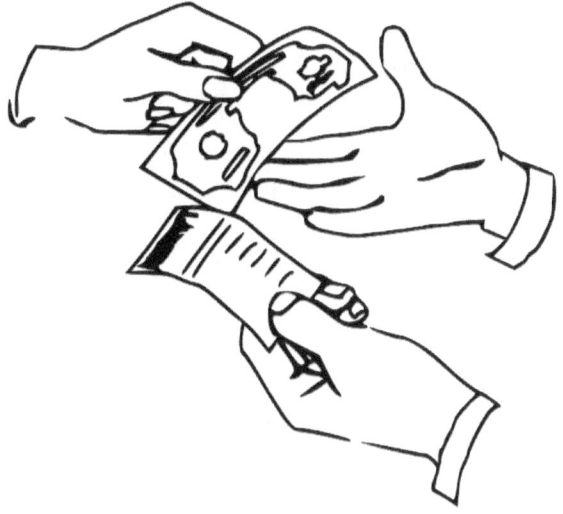

When you meet this buyer, you will know right away that they have what it takes, but in the real sense, they are after a lower price for their offer. They also walk away very fast, especially when the house doesn't do justice for them. They usually have special needs in mind; for instance, they will tell you that they expect the roof to be in a specific way. Failure to give them what they want will make them walk because they know that they have the ability to make things work with their cash.

But the thing for you to remember is that the enticing promise of cold, hard, instant cash is just a way to brag and won't be of a huge benefit to you. So, get ready to drop their desires if the demand is too outrageous.

You need to know that when a buyer decides to get a loan, the money is as good as cash because it will be available for you when you need it.

The Underdog

This buyer is the opposite of the all-cash buyer – they will show you that they have little or no cash for a down payment. The good news is that the buyers usually know what kind of headache they take you, though, so they will be willing to go with your needs as a seller. They know that they aren't in a position to offer a huge down payment, so they will be willing to give in to your demands so that you accept what they have to pay.

The good thing about these buyers is that they are able to close the deal when you agree on the terms.

The Charity Case

These ones are usually so in love with the property that they will submit an offer that is accompanied by a lot of words to show you how they will fit in the property with their pets and all. These are sweet talkers, and they are usually the most rewarding buyers out there. However, you need to remember that the feeling that comes with these buyers won't pay the bills. So, if they don't have a large offer accompanying their words, you need to be ready to move to the next buyer.

You can work with them, but don't let your emotions get the best of you because they have the ability to convince you to take up an offer very fast. Instead, work with them the best way, but make sure you keep your priorities top on the list.

Window Shopper

These buyers are always dreaming of owning a certain home in the future. They believe that when they come and look at the houses available, they will be able to buy one soon. You will hear them talking of "one day I will be in that house." The reality is that these people aren't serious about buying the home at all, t is just a game they are doing.

They will move from property to property, looking at the features and marveling at how the house is good. The chances are that you will meet them often when you are doing your stuff. They will waste your time but are always a good distraction because they will make your day when you realize that nothing is going on.

The Coyote

If your property has been on the market for a long time, you will see this buyer more often. They are looking to see a fault in the property that will make it go for a little lower than what you are asking for. When you meet this type of buyer, you need to be careful so that you don't tell them everything about the property because chances are they will use that against you.

If on the other hand you are out to make a killing and you realize that costs on the property are rising, you can decide to sell it off to this buyer. The good thing is that once you strike an agreement, they will grab the deal fast.

Normal Buyer

This is the person that isn't an expert in the field of real estate. His aim is to get a house to live in. the buyer will search for and locate a property that suits him then go ahead and buy it if it suits him. Such buyers don't have a lot of knowledge in the field and will have only a few deals under their belt.

Agent

The agent is a trader that has knowledge about the area and what happens in the real estate industry. The agent is working on behalf of someone else and usually has about five deals under the belt. Usually, he buys your property, works on it, and then sells it after a few months at a profit of between 10 and 15 percent.

Real Estate Investor

This is the third type of buyer that you will come across. This type of buyer will manage, lead, and control the whole market. They are responsible for the changes in real estate prices. They are looking for a profit that ranges from 100 to 200 percent.

Will Buy Buyers

These are a group of buyers that will buy only when the price is right. They don't need the property so much, but they will only do so if the price is just right. They are looking for bargains and will try to take the price as low as possible. They will make an offer that is way below the market price.

How to Choose the Best Buyer for Your Property

If you live in a real estate market that is hot, you might find that it is easy to receive more than one offer on the sale of the property. You need to understand that the potential buyer is looking up to you to make the decision on whether they have won the deal or not.

You will have to evaluate the various offers in a fair way as you look for the best. Let us look at ways to get the best offer from the multiple ones you receive:

Begin with the Price

The first thing you need to look out for is the price. Normally, any offer that is within your price range should catch your attention, especially when it is above or close to the asking price. However, it doesn't necessarily mean that you hand over the keys to the person with the highest offer.

You might realize that those that offer the most money might be pushing their finances to the limit, and then after the purchase run into trouble.

So, the money shouldn't be the end of the game, try and review the terms of the entire contract before you make a decision. For instance, try and understand how much cash the buyer is throwing in with the home loan before you make a decision.

Compare the Conditions

When a buyer makes an offer, it usually comes with conditions. The fewer the conditions, the better the deal. If you find that the conditions are too many and you cannot manage, then you better cancel the deal however much you were to make from it.

When selling a property, the offers that come with fewer conditions are way better than those that have so many, because the chances of the buyer backing out of the contract are small.

Consider the Value of the Home

When you accept an offer from someone, you need to consider the value of the home as well. For instance, if the price of the property is found to be lower than the original purchase price, then the lending company will not be willing to offer more money to the lender.

When you consider the offers, make sure you understand the value of the home and then see whether the potential buyer has managed to get approved for a loan that is within your needs.

The Closing Periods

If you have a buyer that is willing to close within the week and you have another that will close after two weeks, then the buyer that is willing to close sooner is better than one that will close ages away.

If you wish to move on soon enough, then you may be forced to go with a person that offers a shorter period than one that keeps you waiting months on end.

Look At Extras Offered by Different Buyers

Real estate wholesaling is all about making some profit from a sale for a property as fast as possible. So, if you get a buyer that is willing to add some extras to the deal, the better. For instance, a buyer might offer to pay closing costs, and this will make them stand out from other offers. Another one will offer to overbid the highest bidder by a certain amount, which will be advantageous for you. When considering several offers, then these small bonuses will make things awesome for you.

Get Professional Help

At times, you need to work with a professional to make sure that you get the perfect buyer for your property. In many ways, these professionals have had prior experience with the buyers and know which one will make a purchase or which one won't.

The professional opinion is just there to identify the best buyer, but the ultimate decision stays with you.

Consider their Enthusiasm

When it comes to closing the deal with a buyer, the enthusiasm of a buyer works a lot to tell you that you have a buyer or not. All the homebuyers will look for a house that is best suited for them. Depending on the enthusiasm a certain buyer shows, you will determine whether they are serious or they aren't.

Enthusiasm shows in various ways:

- Honesty
- Response
- Transparency
- Excitement

If a buyer shows that they aren't transparent, you need to be concerned. They could buy the home, but this will turn out to be a red flag for you when selling the property. Buyers that aren't ready to provide the type of information that you need might mean that they are hesitant to buy the property. It can also mean that they aren't able to furnish you with info till a later period.

The response time also shows the level of enthusiasm that they have towards buying the property. If the buyer is just slightly responsive, it means that they are willing to buy the home. If they take some time to respond, and then they might not be willing. This can drag the deal for some time which can make it hard for you to sell the property on time.

A buyer that shows a high level of excitement towards the purchase is always a great sign. However, you need to note whether the excitement is fake or it is genuine. You need to look at the general excitement among all the people because, for instance, a newlywed couple will be excited at all times.

How to Negotiate for a Better Price for Your Property

When you meet with the buyer, you are faced with a dilemma. On one part, you need the buyer to pay a price that you really want so that you make some profit; while on the other hand, the buyer is looking at making sure they don't spend a lot of money on the property.

So, on one side, you will be pushing for a price that is within your range, on the other hand, the buyer is pushing for a price that will leave them something to work with.

Let us look at the strategies to help you get the house on a winning deal:

The Pricing Should Be Right

There is a huge difference between the prices that you wish to get and the price that the market will accept. Remember that the higher the price you set for the property, the harder it will be for you to bargain with the buyer.

You might need to get a certain amount from the property, but remember that a few factors determine the pricing of the house. Let us look at these factors so that you know what you are doing all the time:

- **Location of the property** - when the property is located in a prime place, you will be able to get a good price for it. Location is essentially the proximity to certain amenities and services such as schools, local employment opportunities, and social places.

- **Updates** – while some buyers will be out to find a property that they can fix, most of them usually prefer a house that they can move in immediately. If the house is ready, then you will not bargain for long, but if the house isn't ready for inhabitation, you might find yourself pushing hard to get the deal through.
- **Inspection report** – in some of the markets, the buyers won't be bothered by the inspection report, but this is a risk that the mortgage lender will not forego at all. For many buyers, they need the report for mortgage financing, and when they find that the report isn't available, they will use this as a way to bargain some more.

  So, the presence of an inspection report will greatly impact the price of the property.
- **Comparable properties** – also called comps, these properties that are sold in the area also impact the price of the property. Real estate

agents and appraisers will look at the recent sales of the homes that have similar features so that they can use it as a benchmark when deciding the price.

- **Appraisal value** – this is the formal process s of pricing the property. Every state requires that the property be appraised by a certified organization that is accredited by the right body.

- **The economy** – the value of the property will range according to the economy. So, if the economy is healthy, then you expect the property value to rise.

- **Supply and demand** – simply put, when the demand for property rises, then the price will also increase. If the demand for a particular kind of property is low, then the price will fall.

- **Features** – the features that the property has compared to other properties will make the price go up or down. For instance, if your property has an extra bathroom, then expect the price to go high compared to a property that doesn't have an extra bathroom.

Consider Initial Offers

You need to really pay close attention to the first offer because it might turn out to be the best offer. The best offer for the house usually comes in the initial stages, so don't make a mistake of not listening to the offers, regardless of how and what they are.

Have the Mind of a Salesperson

Before you list the property for sale, you need to make sure you have highlighted the best features of the property to the buyer. When you list the property, make sure you have the mindset of a salesperson – to make the people choose your property first over others.

Avoid Emotions

Many people tend to end up with emotions when buying something, which puts them in a bad situation when it comes to selling as well. When you decide to sell the property, try to avoid the effect of emotions in the process.

Remember that this is business, and it should remain that way till the end. Make sure when you decide that you need a specific price, let it remain that way. Don't be swayed by what the person does or says to make you become emotional.

Try and make decisions based on facts rather than hearsay.

For you to make the right decisions, try and find out how much the buyer has prequalified from the bank for the aim of buying the property. Remember that the more information you have about the needs and the financial situation of the buyer, the better the position you are in when it comes to negotiating.

Stay Realistic

For you to get the best price on your house, you need to stop being stubborn. If the goal is for you to sell, then try and stay realistic. If you feel that the property isn't worth the amount you are trying to sell it for, then don't try to go way above the price just to make more.

You need to come up with the right amount that will allow you to sell the property fast. Remember that when you put an unrealistic value on the property, you will incur extra expenses in terms of insurance, maintenance, utilities, and hard work, with a high risk of theft or vandalism.

Be Creative

When you want to get the best price, you need to exercise ideas that you haven't thought about before. You might even want to throw in a few extras just to make sure things go the right way.

Chapter 10: Closing on The Property

Every process comes with a lot of challenges. Selling a house is challenging and you need to make sure you understand the kinds of challenges that you will come across and how to handle them. Let us look at the different challenges that you will come across.

Poor Quality Images

Many sellers list their property on online platforms with the aim of selling them off to interested buyers. When you take pictures of your online platform, you need to make sure that the picture you choose will show all the features of the property. Remember that the images that you post will either repel or attract a buyer.

Make sure that the images that you take are of high quality. It is always recommended that you get a professional photographer to take the pictures for you. You will spend a little amount, but you will make your life better.

You need to take a lot of images that will show every aspect of the home. Make sure you have pictures of the interior and exterior or part of the home.

Lack of Enough Promotion

Another big challenge that sellers go through is that they don't promote their properties in a good way. Remember that marketing and promotion are a good way to sell your property fast. You can list the property with online agents at a feel, or you come up with your own site to advertise your property.

Talk with an online agent to place a for sale sign in front of the property to increase the chance of attracting buyers fast. The sign will tell people that are passing by that the house is on sale and they will be able to pass the message to interested buyers.

Incorrect Valuation

Another issue with selling the home is finding the perfect valuation. When you value your home the right way, you will be able to sell it at the right price. If you price it at a price that is too high, you might end up not selling it at all. On the other hand, if you price it too low, you might end up selling at a loss.

Valuation of the property is a very important step in selling the house. This is why it is vital that you find the right person to value the house. Make sure you engage various professionals on the same so that you end up with the right valuation.

The good thing is that you can visit online valuation sites that you can use to estimate the property value, or you can also have the estate agent send a local valuation expert to come and provide the needed valuation. Local agents also have a way to identify a good valuation expert, or they will guide you on how to get the right estimate.

Poor Impression

You need to know that first impressions matter when it comes to selling the property. Give your property a good look so before you can put it up for sale. Look at the property and ask yourself whether if you had a chance, you would buy it just by looking at it.

If possible, try and invest some paint and a few simple renovations before you put the property up for sale. You can unclutter the sitting room so that you can make it more presentable. It is also good to know that the people in the area want from the building, and then try to give them what they want.

You Aren't Decided

When you buy a property for resale, you need to have a single mind to sell it;

otherwise, you might find yourself failing to give it away. Many people buy a property then they get attached to it in such a way that they don't get a chance to sell it at all. Remember that if you decide that you don't want the property any longer, you still have to pay the costs of maintenance. Make sure you are ready to sell so that when you place the property on the market, you will let it go. It is frustrating to let a buyer go through the buying process only for you to get out of the deal at the last minute.

Poor Communication

Remember that you might decide to sell the property through a real estate agent that will tell the buyer what you need. You will have to come up with messages that the real estate agent communicates to the buyer. Failure to come up with messages to tell the buyer will result in many things remaining unresolved.

Make sure that you convey messages in a quick and effective way. Don't take weeks to pass across a message that needs to be delivered instantly.

Another big problem with communication is the use of different people to pass different messages at the same time, yet they are for the same property. If you decide to sell, make sure you identify a single real estate agent to handle the communication.

Poor Service

While you need to be able to give proper services to the buyer, you also need to make sure the real estate agent works with your benefit in mind. Let them offer the best service to the buyer so that you can get repeat business later on. You need to give the buyer a good service so that they come back for more. Remember that this isn't the only property you will sell, so make sure you make a name for yourself as the best seller on the market and you will get repeat business the right way.

For you to work with a buyer the right way, make sure you are there when they need to talk to you about business, and you respond to them in a timely manner.

Increasing Rates and Prices

Remember that when you hold onto a property for long, you will end up spending more in terms of the cost of maintaining the house before you sell it. When the rates increase, you will be able to incur more expenses compared to what you had planned for. This way, you find yourself in hot water because it will be hard for you to make the profits that you thought you would make.

Additionally, when the prices of houses increase, you will find it hard to sell to Millenials that are looking for affordable housing solutions.

The Decline In Motivated Buyers

The biggest challenge that you will have as a property seller is to find the right buyer. With the economy changing each day, you will find it tough getting active buyers within your area. New tax plans and other issues that affect the purchasing power of buyers have made it hard for them to keep on buying a property.

This means there is less demand for houses compared to previous years. As much as sales in other markets are increasing, the speed at which they increase isn't as fast as it was before.

Crowded Market

Do you know that you aren't the only seller on the market? When you decide to sell property in a market that is already crowded, you need to be ready for a battle. The market is already full of existing houses, foreclosed homes, and new constructions make it hard for you to get your property going.

When it comes to a crowded market, buyers usually have a huge advantage because they have a lot of property to choose from for their needs. However, when the houses are many, there is high competition from the sellers, and some are willing to add in some extras so that they attract buyers. This will drive the price of the property down, and it will also make it hard for you to sell at your expected price.

High Cost of Repairs

Before you put a house on the market, you need to dedicate some time and money to make sure it is in the best condition. Make sure that you clean and cover up any walls using a fresh coat of paint then replace any carpets that are stained. Many times sellers are tempted to place the house on the market when it isn't ready, but they end up regretting later on. However, buyers won't be inspired by what they will see when they walk around the house. This is why you need to come up with a house that is ready to be inhabited.

Repairing the house is a good idea, but it is expensive. When you look at the cost of equipment and materials on the market, you will realize that you get to spend a lot on the process of repairing the house before you sell it. This cuts deep into your profits.

Finding the Right Agent

One of the biggest challenges in selling a house is to find the right agent to work with. While it makes the whole experience less stressful, you need to make sure that you have the right one; otherwise, the issue will be too tough.

The real estate agent you choose needs to have a few features that will make them the best for your needs:

- Don't choose the agent based on the experience

they have; rather you need to choose someone that you have a good rapport with. Although experience is a good indication to have, it isn't everything. You are going to spend a lot of time with the agent, so you need to really bond. Make sure the person is relatable as well as real. You are choosing the agent for you, not the property. The agent needs to be a good talker and a negotiator as well.

- Look at the chemistry. When you decide to work with an agent, try to look at the chemistry that you have with them. Get a few real estate agents and gauge their honesty and trust, so that you know that you will work well with them.

- Seek referrals. Despite having the technology, you still need real referrals from people that have interacted with real estate agents before. The right referrals need to come from people that are close to you or professional contacts. Ask homeowners which agent they worked with, and then create a list that you can use.

- The real estate agent you choose needs to have your interests at heart all the rime. The agent needs to be transparent and honest about what they are looking to help you achieve, and they will also make sure you get what you go out to in the first place. The agent will try so much to work within your goals and not within his goals. Make sure you ask a lot of questions before you can commit to this professional relationship.

- Follow your gut feeling. When you decide to make

a decision, usually you follow your gut feeling to the latter. This means that you need to meet with a few agents and then follow your gut feeling when it comes to making the right decision. First, look to see if the agent has done business before and if they are recommended by many people. Next, check your gut feeling, if it tells you that things are right, and then this is the right person for the task.

- Trust is vital. Make sure the agent you choose is trustworthy. When you begin a conversation with the agent, try and look at what they answer when you talk to them. Many successful agents have gone to where they are because they are trustworthy. Make sure you have mutual respect and trust between the two of you to work best.

- Passion. Passion drives commitment. When you have an agent that isn't passionate about selling your property, the chances are that you will struggle to find a buyer. On the other hand, if you find an agent that is ready to work with you the right way, then you will see the results fast enough.

- Adequate support. Before you engage a real estate agent, you need to do your research first before you move onto the next thing. When looking at the agent, you need to consider whether they have a team behind them and if they have a customer care team that will respond to your queries and needs. Remember that the agent you are working with doesn't work with you alone – he works with other people as well. And since the logistics of selling a property are daunting, you need to have support all the time.

- Understands risk. You need to work with a real estate agent that understands the risks of selling a house and will throw out any flattery. You want to work with an agent that is realistic about what to expect and is able to mitigate risk in a proper way. Pay close attention to how the agent uses data to tell you about what is happening in the market at all times. The agent needs to tell you about the risk analysis of the decision to buy as well as what to expect in the crowded market that you seek to penetrate.

- Core values. When it comes to making progress with the sale, you need to find a good person that will make sure you enjoy the best experience ever. This boils down to the core values that the agent has – including truthfulness, honesty, and many more.

- Track record. Real estate agents don't just show up out of nowhere; they come from experience and making sure that they do things the right way. Make sure you look at what the top brokers do, then compare to what your agent is doing before you take them up.

Local market Conditions

Before you decide to sell, you need to know that there are a lot of challenges that you need to overcome. These challenges relate to the local market conditions that you have to stick to. The local market conditions usually play a huge role in whether the home will sell or not. Before you decide to sell the home, there are many aspects that you will consider.

- The nature of the market. As a seller, you will have heard of the terms buyer's market or seller's market. A buyer's market is a real estate market where the buyer has a lot of advantages over the sellers. The opposite of this refers to a seller's real estate market. When you decide to sell the property, you need to understand whether you are trading in a seller's market or a buyer's market. The buyer's market is the one where the market is flooded with a lot of listings, and the competition is high. This gives the buyers ample time to get the best property.

- The time of the year also dictates what you do and what you don't do. Remember that every real estate market is different in some way. The time of the year determines the prices and the demand for the properties.

Unrealistic Buyers

We have looked at the types of buyers that you will come across, well they are all ready to buy, but some aren't as serious as others are. There are a lot of ways that today's homebuyers don't become serious with the purchase. You will notice this in various ways that we have discussed earlier in the book. The good thing is that there are many potential buyers that are ready to buy the property when you put it up for sale. They will buy the property, whether it is priced right or not.

Inspections

You need to have an inspection, but at times the need for an inspection is from a buyer that wants to see whether the home passes the test. Buyers have their own aspects that they are looking for, and they will try to make sure that the property passes the test before they can take it up. Since you have already done the inspection, you will expect the buyer to take your word to be true, but most of them don't do this. Instead, they prefer to have their own independent inspector to do the task.

When it comes to a home inspection, there are no set guidelines that tell you that the home has passed the test or failed. This is why it is hard for you to achieve what the buyer is looking for an inspection. For you to get past this nightmare, you need to have a pre-listing inspection that will give you the chance to correct the items that the home inspector finds and will eliminate any challenges.

Closing the Deal

Once you have handled all the other challenges, you expect it to be easy for you to close the deal, right? Well, wrong! Closing the deal is something that needs to be done in a quick and effortless way, but it doesn't happen this way. One of the common issues that can happen before closing the deal is when the buyer gets disapproved. There are many things that a buyer can do that will prevent them from getting approved. This might be out of your hands as a seller, but it is a challenge that you need to overcome so that you move forward.

Final Thoughts

When you have the knowledge that challenges are there when selling the home, you get to make a huge difference. While many of the challenges that arise when selling the home are out of your control, many of them can be controlled easily. Challenges with closing the deal can occur at any time, but when you are sure of what you are doing, these challenges won't happen at all.

www.ingramcontent.com/pod-product-compliance
Lightning Source LLC
Chambersburg PA
CBHW030013190526
45157CB00016B/2578